U.S. NAVY AIR COMBAT
1939—1946

Robert Lawson and Barrett Tillman

MBI Publishing Company

First published in 2000 by MBI Publishing Company, 729 Prospect Avenue, PO Box 1, Osceola, WI 54020-0001 USA

MBI Publishing Company books are also available at discounts in bulk quantity for industrial or sales-promotional use. For details write to Special Sales Manager at Motorbooks International Wholesalers & Distributors, 729 Prospect Avenue, PO Box 1, Osceola, WI 54020-0001 USA.

Library of Congress Cataloging-in-Publication Data available
ISBN 0-7603-1044-0

On the front cover: After early development problems, Vought's F4U-1 Corsair production began in earnest in late 1941. The XF4U-1 reached a level flight speed of 404 miles per hour during 1941, faster than any other Naval fighter of the time. As with the F6F, comparatively few Corsairs were used in the Atlantic theater. The F4U-1A model carries a 500-pound bomb on its centerline rack. *Vought*

On the frontispiece: Marine Scouting Squadron Three Douglas SBD-5 Dauntlesses flying from MCAS Bourne Field, St. Thomas, Virgin Islands, during May 1944. The squadron was one of 15 inshore patrol squadrons assigned to defend East Coast and Caribbean shipping from U-boat attacks. *US Navy*

On the title page and back cover: Credit for being the first squadron to take the Hellcat into combat goes to LCDR Jimmy Flatley's VF-5 when they landed from *Yorktown* (CV-10) on 31 Aug 1943 for strikes against Marcus Is. A CAG 5 Flatley awaits the start signal during the Marcus strikes. *US Navy/LT Charles R. Kerlee*

On the back cover, bottom: Flight decks are one of the most dangerous working environments in the world. On board a training CVE off San Diego, California, (circa 1943) the flight deck bos'n briefs a group of "greenshirts," which include catapult and arresting gear personnel, along with photographers and aircraft technicians. *US Navy*

Printed in China

CONTENTS

Rear Admiral James D. Ramage, USN (Ret)

FOREWORD

LEADERSHIP! THAT WAS THE KEY TO OUR SUCCESS IN World War II. While I am intimately connected with only one ship—USS *Enterprise* (CV-6)—please remember that leaders of stature manned other worthy carriers.

In the prewar era, Annapolis graduates had to serve two years of surface duty prior to flight training. Therefore, when I joined *Enterprise* in 1939, Captain C.A. (Baldy) Pownall was aware of the advice given to Naval Academy graduates to stay clear of aviation because of limited career opportunity. But when he discovered that my roommate, Grant Rogers, and I had requested "The Big E," he said, "You'll never regret coming to this ship." I look back on this as an enormous understatement.

I was assigned as Second Division officer, where the leading petty officer was Boatswain's Mate First Class Van Kuren. I marveled at how he easily handled the 180-man division. Likewise, the ship's Chief Boatswain Filbry was a mentor to me. He emphasized that if you take care of your men, they will go to hell for you.

From an ensign's lowly vantage, I noticed a pattern all the way up the command ladder. The executive officer, the eccentric Commander Felix B. Stump, bore down hard on officers who didn't understand that loyalty was essential to good leadership.

Commander E.C. Ewen was air group commander in 1940, when I was assigned to guide Navy Secretary Frank Knox's tour of the ship. On the flight deck we were met by the CAG, and the secretary remarked that the aircraft were most impressive. At that time the air group consisted of F3F, BT, SBC, and TBD aircraft—half of them biplanes. Ewen's response was, "Mr. Secretary, these planes are not fit to die in." Mr. Knox was taken aback when CAG explained how far we were behind other countries in military aviation. I considered that as a lesson in leadership, as well as telling it like it really is.

During the war itself, Big E personnel consistently demonstrated superb combat leadership. First we must look to the performance of CAG Wade McClusky and skippers Dick Best (VB-6) and Earl Gallaher (VS-6) at Midway. I know of no others who have done more.

After flight training, I was able to wend my way back to *Enterprise*, assigned to VS-10. Commander John Crommelin was ship's exec in 1942–43; the greatest leader whom I have known. His presence in the ready rooms was always exhilarating. Lieutenant Commander Jim Flatley was CO of VF-10, but really was looked upon as CAG because the incumbent in that position was less than forceful. Flatley naturally moved into the job.

Scouting Ten was fortunate in having quiet Lieutenant Commander Bucky Lee as boss. Lieutenant Commander Bill Martin, the initiator of night attack, was exec, while Lieutenant S.B. Strong (whom Flatley considered the bravest man he ever knew) was flight officer. In fact, the arrogant Birney Strong told me that he would make me the second-best dive bomber in the Pacific Fleet! Way down the pecking order was Lieutenant (jg) Red Carmody, who even at that early time showed qualities of leadership.

Commander Roscoe Newman took over as CAG 10 when we went back to the States. I can still hear him emphasizing, "Be good with your primary weapons." He made certain that Air Group Ten was night qualified, which is why *Enterprise* had no fatalities when Task Force 58 lost ninety-seven aircraft the night of 20 June 1944 during the Philippine Sea battle.

Commander Richard Kane, who relieved Newman, was correctly nicknamed "Killer." A quiet man, he let his guns speak for him. Commander Tom Hamilton was ship's exec for our second CAG-10 cruise, carrying on in the Crommelin tradition.

In VB-10 my aircrewman, Radioman First Class Dave Cawley, showed commendable leadership in combat by hand signaling defensive instructions to the other SBDs in formation. These rearseat gunners always deserved our respect.

Then there was the small, quiet man who ran Task Force 58. Vice Admiral Marc Mitscher's presence was felt throughout the force. He was loved and respected, and we knew that he loved us. When he sent us on essentially a one-way mission off Saipan on 20 June, it must have been a difficult decision. But I have never heard a word said against him by any of the participants.

I have briefly described here the leadership and courage that I witnessed in one ship. But there were many carriers and many great warriors, ashore and afloat. This book will tell their story.

Rear Admiral James D. Ramage, USN (Retired)

ACKNOWLEDGMENTS

ACQUISITION OF THE WORLD WAR II NAVAL AVIA-tion color photographs contained in this volume has taken place over a period of 40 years, involving the contributions of a great number of friends, acquaintances, and professional colleagues. Providing a complete listing is difficult and we hope anyone whose name does not appear here will understand the impossibility of recognizing each individual. However, your contribution is appreciated and not forgotten.

The following people have helped make this collection possible: Russ Egnor, director of the Navy's News Photo Division; Bob Carlisle, former head, Navy Still Photo Section; Chris Eckard, Don Montgomery, Dave Parsons, Hal Andrews, Bob Cressman, Doug Siegfried, Lois Lovisolo, Stan Piet, Jay Miller, Harry Gann, Jeff Ethell, and Fred C. Dickey, Jr. Names of other contributors appear in the photo credits.

Grateful recognition is extended to the following publications and individuals for permission to quote portions of their articles or memoirs: Captain Steve Millikin, USN (Retired), editor of *The Hook* magazine; Captain Rosario "Zip" Rausa, USN (Retired), editor of *Wings of Gold* magazine; Captain Earle Rogers, USN (Retired), editor of the Naval Aviation Museum *Foundation;* Mr. Paul Stillwell, director of the US Naval Institute's oral history program in Annapolis, Maryland, and finally Captain T. Hugh Winters, USN (Retired), author of *Skipper: Confessions of a Fighter Squadron Commander.*

To all of the above, and those not listed, a warm thank you.

Robert L. Lawson
Barrett Tillman

PREFACE

THE SECOND WORLD WAR BEGAN WHEN NAZI GERmany invaded Poland in September 1939. The most global of all wars ended when Japan surrendered to the Allies in September 1945. During those six years, US naval aviation expanded by orders of magnitude, fighting a two-ocean war on a scale unimagined only years before.

The United States officially entered the conflict 8 December 1941. On that Monday morning, Congress endorsed President Franklin D. Roosevelt's call that, since the day before, "a state of war has existed between the United States and the Empire of Japan."

The vote was overwhelming, but not unanimous. Montana Representative Jeanette Rankin opposed military action of any kind and opposed American entry into the second global war just as she had opposed entry into the first twenty-four years previously. What recourse she advocated after Japan's surprise attack on the Territory of Hawaii—which left 2,400 American military and civilian dead—can only be surmised.

Three days later Nazi Germany supported the Axis powers by declaring war upon the United States. Adolf Hitler's decision was at least as foolish as it probably was inevitable, but his rare display of support for a marginal ally still has historians shaking their heads in wonder.

The global conflict ended when Italy, Germany, and Japan succumbed to the incredible weight of power brought against them, ending their empires centuries earlier than any one imagined. Italy collapsed in August 1943, Germany surrendered in May 1945, and Japan in September 1945. But diplomats and politicians take little heed of battlefield events. Roosevelt's successor, Harry S. Truman, declared the state of hostilities ended on 31 December 1946. The peace treaty between the United States, Japan, and forty-seven other nations was not signed in San Francisco until 8 September 1951. The new West German government concluded its contract with the Western Allies on 26 May 1952.

More than any before or since, World War II was a naval war. It was hardly surprising; British Prime Minister Winston Churchill and President Roosevelt both had been civilian leaders in their nations' admiralties. Both men had saltwater in their veins, leading to lifelong love affairs with sailing, with navies, and with the sea itself.

But millions of other Americans were swept up in forty-five months of naval combat. From a US population of 134,000,000 the Navy absorbed 3.8 million young men and women; the Marine Corps another 599,693. Of these 4.48 million, 56,683 men were killed in action; 30,422 died of other causes; and 104,985 were wounded: more than 190,000 American families were affected by sons killed, missing, or injured in prosecuting a two-ocean war.

Despite a universal draft, 38.8 percent of all American servicemen in World War II were volunteers. For a variety of reasons—physical, mental, or emotional—more than one-third of all men examined for induction were rejected for military service.

The average serviceman spent thirty-three months in uniform, and nearly three in four went overseas. Those individuals typically spent sixteen months outside the continental US. Average base pay for all enlisted men was $71.33 per month; for officers, $203.50. The hazardous-duty bonus, such as for aircrew and submariners, added 50 percent to base pay.

For many of those sailors, aviators, or Marines, World War II was the defining experience of their lives. For the majority, it was at the very least inconvenient; for many others it brought upheaval, separation from hearth and home, and months or years of oppressive tedium. After all, the reality of Navy service in the Second World War was more typically reflected by the motion picture *Mr. Roberts* than by *Flying Leathernecks*.

But for some, World War II remains the landmark event in their achievement of not only maturity, but of their self-identity. As one fighter pilot said in 1995, "I was never happier than when I was in combat. I'd do it again tomorrow."

Another aviator expressed it differently, saying, "I wouldn't take a million dollars for the experience. But you couldn't pay me that much to do it again!"

Good, bad, or indifferent, the war's effect upon those who survived naval aviation's greatest challenge marked them for life. This is their story.

FROM THE GOLDEN AGE INTO DARKNESS

Between June 1940 and December 1941 (US) military expenditures exceeded those of World War I. Metal was being pounded into weapons as though every day mattered, which it did. The Depression was over. The national defense program ended it, while the New Deal had failed to do much more than pass a limp hand over the gaunt visage of hunger.
Geoffrey Perret,
A Country Made by War

IN JUNE 1939, THE US NAVY COUNTED 1,277 AIRCRAFT deployed in Atlantic or Pacific Fleet units. Of these, 371 were assigned to America's six aircraft carriers, including forty-three liaison or utility types which were carrier-capable but had no combat function.

Excluding the hodge-podge of utility (VJ) birds, the carrier air groups comprised six primary combat types: Grumman F2F/F3F biplane fighters; Curtiss SBC and Vought SBU biplane scout bombers; Vought SB2U and Northrop BT monoplane dive bombers; and Douglas TBD monoplane torpedo planes. It is significant that, on the verge of the Second World War, the US Navy's carrier air groups were 27 percent biplanes.

One of the most numerous fleet types was the Curtiss SOC, a scout-observation biplane usually flown as a floatplane but capable of wheeled undercarriage. Nearly 170

USS *Enterprise* (CV-6) makes ready for flight quarters while underway in the Pacific during mid-late 1941. At the outbreak of America's entry into WWII, the Navy had seven aircraft carriers in commission. *Langley* (CV-1) had been converted in 1937 to a seaplane tender. *US Navy*

were distributed throughout battleship and cruiser divisions as well as various administrative staffs.

Patrol aviation was largely the province of Consolidated's PBY, a twin-engine flying boat which would prove exceptionally long-lived. Some 190 equipped two complete patrol wings and part of two more. The slack was taken up by antiquated but still useful P2Y biplanes, also built by Consolidated.

Therefore, with a modern European war only three months away, the Navy's air arm was very much a weapon in transition. On 1 June the Bureau of Aeronautics was turned over to Rear Admiral John H. Towers, only the third US naval officer to earn his wings. A gifted administrator, Jack Towers, was the right man in the right place at the right time.

Ninety days later the world went to war for the second time in twenty-one years.

World War II in Europe began with Germany's invasion of Poland on 1 September 1939. Four days later President Roosevelt issued a declaration stating US neutrality and the nation's intent to enforce that stance. It was both inaccurate and optimistic, for the president was strongly pro-British and the US armed forces were ill-pre-

A Curtiss SBC-4 Helldiver from Naval Reserve Air Base (NRAB) New York, c. 1940–41. First introduced to the fleet in 1937, the SBC was assigned to both fleet and Naval Reserve units at the outbreak of the war. VMSB-151 flew SBC-4s until June 1943. The SBC was also the last operational biplane in carrier service. On the verge of WWII, the Navy's carrier groups were still composed of 27 percent biplanes. *Rudy Arnold/NASM*

pared for war. But, in the face of popular isolationist sentiment, Roosevelt considered the sham necessary for political reasons.

The Navy was ordered to establish the Neutrality Patrol to 300 nautical miles off the East Coast, running southward along the boundary of the Caribbean Sea. Any foreign warships entering the zone were to be reported immediately.

On paper Rear Admiral A.W. Johnson's Atlantic Squadron had a reasonably-imposing organization to "enforce" the patrol: four battleships, five cruisers, forty or more destroyers, and two aircraft carriers; USS *Ranger* (CV-4) and the new

Wasp (CV-7). The battleships' aviation element was Observation Squadron Five (VO-5), while the cruisers embarked elements of Observation-Scouting Squadron Seven (VOS-7).

However, the bulk of actual patrolling would be conducted by five flying-boat squadrons supported by four tenders. In all, thirty-six Consolidated PBY-1, -2s, and -3s and eighteen older P2Y-2s were based at Newport, Rhode Island; Norfolk, Virginia; and in Cuba and Puerto Rico. Detachments were also sent to Charleston, South Carolina, and Key West, Florida.

Whatever Franklin Roosevelt's faults as commander-in-chief, he was devoted to the Navy. Therefore, with an eye toward

Following a 1939 contract from the Navy, Curtiss produced another "Helldiver," the monoplane SB2C. XSB2C-1 BuNo 1758 was first flown 18 Dec 1940. *Rudy Arnold, courtesy Stan Piet*

eventual American involvement in the global war, his administration pushed through the Two-Ocean Navy Act in July 1940. Nothing had been seen like it in American history. Aircraft strength went from 1,741 on hand to an authorized level of 15,000. Naval construction likewise soared, with entire new classes of combatant and support vessels. Personnel requirements escalated accordingly.

The effect of America's defense program upon an economy still recovering from the Great Depression was startling. In fact, the onset of World War II was actually what turned the nation around; Roosevelt's social programs still had not cured the economy after seven years of Fair Deal politics. Unemploy-

ment in 1940 was nearly 15 percent, but never fully disappeared. As one naval aviator noted a half-century later, "Even at the height of the war in 1943, with full mobilization, we still had 2 percent unemployment. That's because at least 2 percent of the population is unemployable!"

Administrative changes accompanied the unaccustomed windfall. The Pacific Fleet was established 1 February 1941 with Admiral Husband E. Kimmel in command at Pearl Harbor, Hawaii. He would remain at the helm until December of that year. The Atlantic Fleet, headquartered at Norfolk, Virginia, was entrusted to astute, acerbic Admiral Ernest J. King. As both a submariner and aviator, he was uncommonly well pre-

Above
Yorktown's (CV-5) Scouting Five SBD-3 Dauntlesses in 1940–41 all-gray paint scheme. Arguably WWII's finest dive bomber, the Dauntless was developed from the Northrop BT-1, and SBD-2s began fleet service in 1940 with VB- and VS-6 on board *Enterprise* (CV-6) while all SBD-1s went to the Marines. *Douglas, courtesy Harry Gann*

Left
Douglas' TBD Devastator was the US Navy's first carrier-based monoplane, initially serving with Torpedo Three in *Saratoga* (CV-3) in 1937. VS-42 TBD-1 assigned to *Ranger* (CV-4) wears the overall-gray paint scheme of 1940-41. *Rudy Arnold/NASM*

Above
Northrop BT-1 off the coast of Southern California during 1939 in spurious "Hi-Hatter" markings of *Ranger's* (CV-4) VB-4. The aircraft is actually assigned to *Yorktown's* (CV-5) VB-5 and was specially painted for the movie *"Dive Bomber."* Courtesy Stan Piet

Right
Wearing the willow green tail markings assigned to *Ranger* (CV-4) and a neutrality patrol insignia on its cowling, this Vought SBU-1 served with VS-41 in the Atlantic during 1941. *CAPT Brainard McComber, USN(Ret), courtesy John Lundstrum*

Brewster F2A-3 Buffalo, off the East Coast during 1941. Although the F2A won a competition against Grumman's F4F Wildcat to become the Navy's first monoplane fighter, it achieved little success and served the Navy operationally only with VF-2 and -3 on board *Lexington* (CV-2) and *Saratoga* (CV-3), respectively, as well as briefly with VS-201 on board *Long Island* (ACV-1). Marine Fighter Squadron 221 flew the Brewster's only US combat and was nearly annihilated at the Battle of Midway. *NASM*

pared to deal with the complexities of modern naval warfare. King's star would ascend almost as fast as Kimmel's fell.

A contingency organization, the Support Force Atlantic Fleet, was established in March 1941 with destroyers and a five-squadron patrol wing. Directed to prepare for operations in northern waters, the patrol crews practiced convoy escort and antisubmarine warfare. The intent was to prevent German commerce raiders and U-boats from interrupting USA-UK shipping routes.

Elements of VP-52 arrived at Argentia, Newfoundland, in May 1941 with the tender *Albemarle* (AV-5). The conditions were wretched: horrible weather, poor communications, and meager facilities. On 24 May, just six days after the Catalinas arrived, came news that the German battleship *Bismarck* had sunk HMS *Hood* in the Denmark Strait between Iceland and Greenland. Eleven VP-52 aircraft took off to search for the raider but became lost and scattered. It was days before they all returned to Argentia.

Bismarck had turned southeast after her victory over the British battlecruiser, but could not evade detection

much longer. And American aviators were actively involved in finding her.

Seventeen PBY pilots had been sent to Britain in April to instruct Royal Air Force Coastal Command in Catalina operations. The effectiveness of some instructors was openly doubted by the fliers themselves, as some were fresh-caught ensigns with merely thirty hours in type.

Nevertheless, the Navy pilots began flying search missions with Coastal Command squadrons. One such was Ensign Leonard B. Smith, assigned to No. 209 Squadron at Lough Erne, Northern Ireland. Upon news of *Hood's* loss, Smith found himself airborne on his second mission with the RAF, flying with the crew of Pilot Officer Briggs.

Arriving in the search area eight hours after takeoff, "Tuck" Smith looked ahead and slightly to starboard. He hardly believed his eyes: there, perhaps five miles away, was the dark, brooding silhouette of a battleship. Slipping closer for visual confirmation at 2,800 feet, the Catalina was spotted. All doubt as to the battleship's identity was removed when she opened accurate fire at the flying boat. Smith stood the ungainly PBY on a wingtip, scooting for the safety of nearby clouds.

Smiths' and Briggs' crew tracked *Bismarck* for the next four hours, awaiting relief. Each of the next two PBYs on station also had an American pilot aboard. When the British battleship-cruiser force caught and destroyed the raider, naval airpower received a boost. Patrol planes had found *Bismarck*, and Royal Navy carrier aircraft had slowed her with a torpedo hit.

VMF-121 Grumman F4F-3 Wildcat in factory-fresh paint during 1941. In late 1939 the Corps had but nine squadrons assigned to two aircraft groups and 1,383 men in aviation billets. *NASM*

SB2U-3 Vought Vindicator (sometimes called "wind indicator") assigned to VMSB-131, Marine Air Group 11, on the West Coast during 1940–41. The SB2U was the Navy's first monoplane scout bomber, reporting to the fleet with VB-3 in December 1937. *NASM, courtesy Jeff Ethell*

American and British cooperation extended well beyond occasional operational sorties such as the *Bismarck* hunt. Joint scientific research from radar to the atomic bomb became significant projects, and US Navy personnel usually were involved in some degree. One of the most far-reaching programs for naval aviation involved shipboard radar.

Coaching the Fighters

Henry A. Rowe was a 1937 Annapolis graduate who won his wings in 1940. He went to Britain to study radar in 1941 and spent most of the war as an embarked fighter direction officer (FDO) or instructor. He saw the program evolve into a highly sophisticated, technically advanced method of fleet defense, which began from humble prewar origins. Some of his observations follow:

After I returned from my tour with the British Fleet Air Arm, I told Rear Admiral Ofstie how much better the Brits were with RDF (radio direction finding) aboard their carriers than we were. I returned to Washington the day before Pearl Harbor, and it was obvious that we would need well-trained officers and men for combat information centers (CICs), including FDOs.

We felt that a good fighter director was a manager rather than a pilot or technical scientist. What you're doing is managing a bunch of fighters. You have an input of so many planes, how long they can fly at climb or at altitude, when you can get them back aboard ship and so on.

Left
LSO directs VF-42 Grumman F4F-3 Wildcat pilot during an FCLP (Field Carrier Landing Practice) drill. The F4F was Grumman's first monoplane fighter. *US Navy*

Below
Development of Martin's successful PBM Mariner series began in 1937 with initial deliveries going to VP-55 and -56 at NAS Norfolk in 1941. *Rudy Arnold, courtesy Stan Piet*

Martin was less successful with its XPB2M-1 Mars follow-on to the PBM. At the time the world's largest aircraft, XPB2M-1 development began in 1938 and first flight came 3 July 1942. Converted to a transport, the ex-patrol bomber became the XPB2M-1R. Subsequent versions were the JRM-1 and -2 Mars, of which a total of six were built. *NASM*

By the time the United States entered the war, development of Consolidated's PBY Catalina had progressed to the -5A model. Twenty-five patrol squadrons were flying various models of the PBY by the end of 1941. *Rudy Arnold, courtesy Stan Piet*

So what does it take? Well, it takes somebody who can think on his feet, keep account of all that is going on that affect an air battle, and don't get bound up with one small corner of the problem. I saw some Brit pilot FDOs who would try to take over flying the plane they were directing and ignore other bogies that were coming in. So managing a resource is what you're concerned with.

We could have anybody we wanted, so we decided that anybody who made over $30,000 in the past three years, entirely on his own, none inherited, was probably good and sharp. We had a lot of lawyers and stock brokers, just a good group of fairly young guys. One of them was John Connally, who was one of the finest nonpilot FDOs we ever had.

We set up a fighter director school at St. Simon Island, Georgia, and later there were other places in the United States and in Hawaii. We tried to have a few pilots as fighter-direction officers (FDOs), but for the masses you needed in amphibious operations, for convoys and so on, you had nonpilots. Otherwise you wouldn't have any pilots left.

The Luftwaffe used more pilots than we did, and after the war I spent some time in NATO and ran across some German fighter pilots. They tried to swap them back and forth but there was not a lot to be gained by having a pilot in the job, particularly if you put him there because he wasn't a good pilot. If he wasn't psychologically suited to be flying, he wasn't suited to be controlling a plane, either. However, working on a one-to-one basis with a night fighter, sometimes there were advantages to having a good aviator on the scope.

Additionally, once people such as Jack Griffin and myself saw how hard it was to get back into flying, they tended to stay away from the FDO program. The only way I got back was by convincing the wheels that we needed an airborne fighter director over the fleet to extend the radar horizon, so I checked out in a B-17 and that became the PB-1W which led the way to the postwar "Willy Victor" program.

We developed a doctrine for dealing with enemy air attacks that was composed of a few points. First, no raid shall come in unopposed. Use sufficient force to break up and destroy enemy coordination, with complete destruction of enemy force being highly desirable. Intercept at maximum range consistent with good radio communications and good radar information. If possible, keep enough reserve fighters over base for backing up the engaged fighters and dealing with new attacks.

There were tactical considerations for the directors, too. They wanted to keep up a line of patter with the lead pilots so they knew what the weather and visibility was. Condensation trails would give our planes away at specific altitudes; it's nothing to see contrails at 50 miles. In the summer they're higher than in the winter. So we wanted to bring our fighters out of the sun, and give them an altitude advantage.

Rowe wrote the Pacific Fleet Radar Center FDO manual in early 1945 and subsequently served with the British Pacific Fleet during the Okinawa campaign. After the war, he took a three-year advanced course in electronics, retiring in 1965.

Operational with fleet units 1930-35, the Curtiss O2C was relegated to the Reserve until 1938. NRAB Floyd Bennett O2C-1 taxis for takeoff. *Fred E. Bamberger*

Anglo-American cooperation continued that summer as six new Martin PBM-1s of VP-74 and six PBY-5s of VP-73 moved to Iceland's Skerja Fjord in August. Though supported by tender *Goldsborough* (APD-32), the "P-boats" also used RAF moorings. Spartan accommodation and facilities rendered Iceland a hardship duty post, but aerial patrol range was considerably extended.

Meanwhile, US Navy men were increasingly embroiled in the European war. In July 1941, American warships started escorting British merchantmen to and from Iceland, and beginning 1 September that duty was broadened to trans-Atlantic convoys, as one British historian observed, "on the disingenuous grounds that they included ships bound for Iceland."

Two shooting incidents quickly resulted. On 4 September, the destroyer *Greer* (DD-145) was steaming independently for Iceland when she received a message from a British aircraft: an unidentified submarine had dived 10 miles ahead. *Greer* established sonar contact, but after three hours of uneventful tracking, the RAF plane was low on fuel and optimistically dropped depth charges in the area before leaving.

Right
Vought's remarkable OS2U Kingfisher joined the fleet with VO-4 during August 1940 and served as a front-line observation aircraft until the end of the war. Three OS2U-1s of Battleship Division 3 in colorful prewar paint schemes during 1940. *NASM*

The U-boat skipper logically assumed that his stalker had finally attacked and fired two torpedoes at the destroyer. Both missed. *Greer* counterattacked, also missed, and the both combatants disengaged.

It might have ended there, but President Roosevelt publicly described the event as German "piracy." Soon after he declared that German and Italian naval vessels entering the Western Atlantic would do so at their own peril. Rules of engagement were amended to a shoot-on-sight basis, placing the US Navy in an undeclared war with Germany.

The secret conflict expanded the next month. In the last half of October, two US Navy destroyers and an oiler were torpedoed by U-boats. Two ships survived. But the second destroyer, *Reuben James* (DD-245), was tagged while escorting

Convoy HX-156. She sank fast, losing 115 of her crew, including every officer.

Meanwhile, Admiral Towers had worked diligently to upgrade naval aviation for the coming war. By July 1941 the Navy counted nearly 3,500 aircraft, of which half were judged combat-capable, with contracts amounting to as many more in the next fiscal year. The BuAer planners expected aircraft acquisition to double again between July 1942 and July 1943.

Three carriers participated in the Neutrality Patrol, usually operating from Norfolk, Virginia. *Ranger* (CV-4), *Yorktown* (CV-5), and *Wasp* (CV-7) made periodic forays into the Atlantic and Caribbean, but in truth the sorties were more training exercises than operational deployments.

Marine Corps aviation also expanded during the two years prior to December 1941. In late 1939, the Corps possessed nine squadrons deployed in two aircraft groups with 1,383 men in aviation billets. At the time of Pearl Harbor only four more squadrons had been added, but a wing structure had evolved and total aviation personnel had grown to nearly 6,500. The expansion was overseen by Brigadier General Ralph J. Mitchell, who remained director of Marine Corps Aviation until early 1943.

Accustomed to making do with cast-off Navy aircraft, the Marines received a pleasant surprise in 1940. Marine Bombing Squadron One at Quantico, Virginia, accepted the first Douglas SBD-1 scout bombers and immediately set about learning how to employ such modern aircraft. The Navy's initial Dauntlesses (as they were named in late 1941) were SBD-2s with greater internal fuel capacity.

The Delightful Dauntless

Lieutenant Commander Harry Don Felt was skipper of Bombing Two when the squadron received the fleet's first SBD-2s. He flew the Douglas scout-bombers for the next three years and came to appreciate the prewar preparation when the targets shot back.

I find an entry in my flight log dated 27 December 1940 of having flown SBD-2 No. 2105. Flipping the pages, I see that 2105 and I together had a ball. I had command of VB-2 from mid-1939 to the end of 1941. We were the first to be assigned SBD-2s, and it appears that 2105 was first in the barn.

At any rate, during the ensuing years we were separated only when she was in for maintenance. Lexington was our home at sea, and when based temporarily ashore, we were at North Island (San Diego), Ford Island in Hawaii, and at Lake Charles, Louisiana, for Army maneuvers. We participated in a

The Marines planned to expand their 1941 glider force from 75 gliders and 150 pilots to a 1942 estimate of 1,370 aircraft and nearly 3,500 pilots; enough to lift 10,800 combat-ready Marines. However, by May 1943 the program was canceled. Marine pilots are in a Schweizer LNS-1 c. 1942. *US Navy, courtesy Stan Piet*

Right
USCG JF-2 pilot warms up engine as enlisted crewmember mans rear cockpit. During 1934–41 the Coast Guard operated 14 Grumman JF-2 Ducks, replacing them in 1942 with J2F-5/6s. *Rudy Arnold, courtesy Stan Piet*

VMB-2 Douglas SBD-1 Dauntless is on a factory delivery flight over Los Angeles in late 1940. All 56 SBD-1s served with Marine Corps squadrons VMB-1 and -2. *Douglas, courtesy Harry Gann*

Utility Squadron Four (VJ-4) mechs perform maintenance on Sikorsky JRS-2 amphibian at NRAB Squantum, Mass. Prewar VJ squadrons (changed to VU in 1946, then VC in 1965) performed vital service missions to the fleet such as target towing, gunnery calibration and photo mapping. *US Navy*

two-day attack on Oahu in May 1941, demonstrating to the Japanese consul general, resident cross channel from Ford Island, how it could be done.

My last flight with 2105 was from Lex to Ford Island where, on 28 December, I was relieved of command of VB-2. On the 29th an SBD took me to Saratoga. But she was torpedoed on 11 January and went to Bremerton for repairs. My air group was split—part of it remaining at Pearl and my part ferrying to North Island to assist training backup pilots and crewmen.

Another SBD and I were inseparable while I was Sara's CAG. BuNo 03213 acquired the name "Queen Bee" and kept on flying for many months after Sara's second torpedo (31 August 1942). While in Operational Training Command at Daytona Beach, I received a letter informing me that "Queen Bee" had suffered too many wounds and had been put to rest over the side with appropriate ceremony.

Flying "Queen Bee," Felt led the attack which sank the Japanese carrier *Ryujo* at the Eastern Solomons battle. Rising to

Four Douglas R3D-2 transports were procured for Marine Corps paratroop training in 1940. VMJ-152 was based at Quantico, Va., at the time. *US Navy, courtesy Jeff Ethell*

four stars, he commanded US Pacific Forces during the 1960s, and died in Honolulu in 1992.

Despite some new equipment, biplanes remained in the Marine inventory for many months to come. Fighter transition from Grumman F3Fs to F4Fs and Brewster F2As took a while, and Curtiss SBCs served in Pacific rear areas until well into 1942.

Gliders captured the interest of military planners after Germany's success at Crete in May 1941. Marine plans grew from seventy-five gliders and 150 pilots to a 1942 estimate of 1,370 aircraft and nearly 3,500 pilots and copilots: enough to lift 10,800 combat-ready Marines. However, reality dictated otherwise, and the program died a lingering death, finally expiring in May 1943.

An aviation-related program which came closer to fruition was the Marine Corps parachutists. Though intended for airborne operations, the few companies of paratroopers fought while attached to one of the two Marine raider battalions.

One group of aviators who did get to combat ahead of their contemporaries was the American Volunteer Group. Recruited from active-duty American military personnel, the AVG was established by agents of the US and Chinese governments during 1941. Of nearly 100 pilots, fifty-five were Navy or Marine Corps aviators. Though some had never flown fighters, they were drilled in Colonel Claire Chennault's tactics flying P-40Bs and helped defend the Burma Road supply line against the Japanese.

"We Didn't Know What We Were Getting Into"

John R. "Dick" Rossi was a part-time student and mer-

chant sailor who was accepted for Navy flight training in 1939. Hoping for an overseas assignment after graduation, he was disappointed to become a "plowback" instructor at Pensacola. Therefore, he jumped at the chance to join the AVG.

I arrived back in San Francisco aboard SS President Garfield in early 1939 and, though underweight, I submitted my application to the Navy with two letters of recommendation. Not being very optimistic about my chances, I applied also to Pan American Airways for a job as purser on their Clippers.

August arrived and I had heard nothing, so I went over to Berkeley and signed up for the fall term. Just before school was to start, I received a notice from the Navy to report to Oakland Reserve Base for a physical. The mail also brought a notice to report to Pan American on Treasure Island. I set my priorities; if that did not work out, I would go to Pan Am; failing that, I would go back to school.

I reported for my Navy physical and, though still underweight, I was given an NCD (not considered disqualified). However, I was ordered to report to the dispensary after every meal to drink an ounce of cod liver oil. I took a lot of ribbing from the other aspiring cadets about that. Our elimination training started in September.

Our class reported to Pensacola the last week of December 1939, and we started our flight training in January 1940 as Class

Another Marine Corps program was designed to train parachutists to operate with Marine Raider battalions. Parachutists train at Camp Kearny, near San Diego, California, in front of a VMJ-152 Douglas R3D-2 transport. *US Navy*

134C. After getting my commission and wings, I was ordered to the newly opened Saufley Field as an instructor at Squadron 1C. I remained there until August 1941 when, in the old San Carlos Hotel, I signed up to go to China with Central Aircraft Manufacturing Company (CAMCO) in the American Volunteer Group, which would become known to history as the Flying Tigers.

We were required to resign our commissions due to the nature of the job and proper relations with Japan. The contract was for one year with assurance that we could return to the Navy in our old slot with no loss of seniority. The Pearl Harbor attack altered the future plans of all the volunteers in the group.

After checking out of Pensacola, we were all instructed to report to the CAMCO representative at San Francisco for passage to China. We were told that we would be a fighter group flying P-40s, and that our mission would be to protect the Burma Road; that we would be followed by a bomber group and then another fighter group. Our group was named the First American Volunteer Group (FAVG), but the second and third never formed. We didn't have much information and really didn't know what we were getting into.

In San Francisco, the Pensacola contingent of eighteen pilots was joined by more Navy and Army pilots, plus some ground support personnel. Most of the FAVG had already departed, which made our group the last contingent of pilots to

Second production Grumman F4F-3 Wildcat BuNo 1845, is on a test flight during summer 1940. Although the F4F initially lost out to Brewster's F2A because of a slightly lower max speed, the Wildcat soon proved to be the superior fighter and was the naval service's mainstay for the first year and a half of the war. *Rudy Arnold, courtesy Hal Andrews*

Grumman's magnificent Avenger torpedo bomber was first flown as the XTBF-1 on 7 Aug 1941 by Grumman test pilot Bob Hall. XTBF-1 BuNo 2539, seen here in its only known color photo, was lost 28 Nov 1941 as a result of an in-flight fire. The flight test crew successfully parachuted from the aircraft. *Grumman, courtesy H.L. Schonenberg*

VMF-111 Grumman F4F-3A Wildcats wear "Orange Force" cross markings during August 1941 war games conducted in South Carolina. *US Navy*

Grumman's initial attempt to produce a twin-engine fighter for the Navy was its XF5F-1 Skyrocket. Only one example was built, BuNo 1442, completed in March 1940. Interestingly, the Skyrocket was used as the aircraft for the comic book character "Blackhawk's" squadron. *Grumman, courtesy H.L. Schonenberg*

arrive in Rangoon. Several additional ground support people arrived on a later ship.

We sailed from San Francisco on 24 September 1941 on the Dutch ship, MS Boschfontein, arriving in Rangoon on 12 November. That afternoon we boarded the train for Toungoo, Burma, which was to be our temporary training base. With our arrival, the FAVG was essentially complete except for the half-dozen support people behind us.

We arrived in Toungoo, about 170 miles north of Rangoon, about 2200. Some of the volunteers who had

Photo taken during August 1941 South Carolina war games depicts early-style oxygen system used by Wildcat pilots. Pilot and aircraft are from either VMF-111 or VF-8, flying both F4F-3s and -3As. *NASM*

Left
Section of VF-5 Grumman F4F-3A Wildcats during 1941. The F4F-3A was powered by an R-1830-90 single-stage supercharged engine as opposed to the straight-3's R-1830-76 or R-1830-86. *Rudy Arnold, courtesy Lois Lovisolo*

Dressed in *Ranger's* (CV-4) willow green tail markings, this factory-fresh Grumman F4F-3 Wildcat has yet to receive its full markings of VF-42 while on a February 1941 test flight. Prior to WWII, naval aircraft were normally delivered in full squadron markings painted by the manufacturers. *Courtesy Richard M. Hill*

arrived before us came down from the base to meet us. We all saw people whom we knew, but had no idea they had joined the AVG also.

Having been raised in an Italian ancestry family of ten children, I thought I was pretty used to chaos. I later realized that we had been fairy well organized in comparison to some outfits I later joined. Things in Toungoo did not run all that smoothly.

Since our group of pilots on the Boschfontein *was the last to arrive, we were months behind the first arrivals. They had already had months of lectures from Chennault and many hours of indoctrination in the P-40, plus gunnery, formation, and dogfighting practice.*

Many things had happened before our arrival, including a couple of fatal accidents, resignations, and training accidents, resulting in the loss of quite a few P-40s. The first few of our group to get P-40 flight time managed a couple more accidents. Chennault was very agitated and cancelled P-40 checkouts for new arrivals until they had an indoctrination flight in the group's BT-9 (or the NJ as we Navy called it.) Unfortunately, the NJ was out of commission so our checkouts were delayed.

More than a week passed before I was able to get a couple of hops in the NJ and then try my hand at the P-40. Our cockpit checkout and instructions came from an ex-Navy pilot, Edgar "Eddie" Goyette. The first P-40 flight was uneventful but certainly different. After almost a year instructing in N3Ns, the P-40 was quite an experience. One of my main motivations for joining the AVG was to get into combat-type planes. The P-40 definitely fulfilled that desire; it required full attention to keep it under control.

On Monday morning, 8 December (we were on the other side of the international date line), first came rumors and then confirmation of the attack on Pearl Harbor. We were both shocked and jubilant. There was always the danger of a Japanese attack on the United States, but it was a big surprise that the first US target would be Pearl Harbor. Now our presence had a double purpose. We would be fighting directly for the United States as well as our allies.

Rossi flew with the AVG's First Pursuit Squadron and was credited with 6.25 enemy aircraft. When the Flying Tigers were disbanded in July 1942, he joined China National Aviation Corporation, flying transport aircraft "over the hump" from India into China.

CHAPTER
TWO

THE ATLANTIC PALL

"The Atlantic," Adolf Hitler had said, "is my first line of defense in the West." Only the breaking of
that sea line made possible the great Allied land offensives.
Richard Hanser,
Victory at Sea

ON 7 DECEMBER 1941, USS *WASP* LAY AT ANCHOR OFF Bermuda, enjoying shore leave under "holiday routine" when the stunning news was received from Hawaii. No better indication of the peacetime Navy's mindset is available than the fact that no recall to the ship was instituted. Recalled one ensign, "We just went on partying like normal." Hitler's Germany finally formalized the de facto reality and declared war on America on 11 December. Though the abysmal litany of defeat in the Pacific captured the public's attention, carriers and naval aviation were active in the European and Mediterranean Theaters early on.

First into the European war was *Wasp*, which left the East Coast in late March 1942 and arrived at the Royal Navy anchorage at Scapa Flow on 4 April. Loading forty-seven Supermarine Spitfires to reinforce the Mediterranean island of Malta, *Wasp* conducted her first delivery on 20 April: she flew off a combat air patrol (CAP) of Grumman F4F-3s, then launched the British

VGS-29 Grumman TBF-1 Avenger is brought to the flight deck on *Santee's* (ACV-29) forward elevator during August 1942. *Santee* joined the Atlantic ASW forces and scored its first U-boat kill in July 1943. *US Navy*

fighters when within range of the island. The flattop returned to Scapa Flow six days later.

But Malta's garrison air force suffered high attrition, owing to continuous Axis bombing. A second reinforcement trip began 2 May with forty-seven more Spitfire Mk Vs flown off 9 May.

One of the Spitfires crashed on takeoff, and *Wasp* ran over the wreckage. All the others got off safely. But soon after launch, Canadian pilot, Pilot Officer J.A. Smith found he was unable to transfer fuel from his auxiliary tank. Unable to reach Malta, he waited for the launch to finish, then entered the landing pattern. The sailors were amazed: the hookless Spitfire was coming aboard!

The LSO was Lieutenant David McCampbell, who rushed to the platform with his paddles. Smith's initial approach was too high so McCampbell waved him off.

On his next attempt, Smith did better. He was "fast in the groove" but McCampbell compensated by giving the "cut" signal earlier than normal. As the Spit touched down, the young Canadian stood on the brakes and lurched to a stop about 6 feet from the end of the deck.

Plane captain assists Helldiver pilot prior to launch from *Yorktown* (CV-10) during her shakedown off Trinidad in mid-1943. *US Navy*

That evening Dave McCampbell gave Jerry Smith a spare pair of Navy wings, with a suitably decorated cake to mark the occasion. Much later, *Wasp* learned that Pilot Officer Smith disappeared chasing enemy aircraft on 10 August.

It was this cruise which prompted Winston Churchill's quip, "Who said a wasp can't sting twice?"

Wasp returned to the United States almost immediately, preparing for deployment to the Pacific.

Ranger also ferried fighter aircraft to distant shores, but they were USAAF Curtiss P-40s rather than RAF Spitfires. She delivered sixty-eight Warhawks to Africa's Gold Coast in April, followed by a second run in June.

VS-41 Douglas SBD-3 Dauntless comes aboard *Ranger* (CV-4) 6 Sep 42. Scouting 41 transitioned to SBD-3s just two months before taking them into combat during Operation Torch 8 Nov 1942. *US Navy*

Famed for his exploits as a fighter pilot and Commander Air Group 15, where he finished the war as the Navy's leading fighter ace with 34 kills, Dave McCampbell (CAPT, USN Ret) was *Wasp's* (CV-7) landing signal officer during the early days of the war. Personnel seen here with LT McCampbell are ENS George E. "Doc" Savage (behind), Len Ford (in dungarees), and LT Hawley Russell (foreground). *US Navy, courtesy Russ Egnor*

But ferry runs were peripheral duties. The abiding concern in the Atlantic was the ongoing war against German submarines, which threatened to sever communications between the New World and the Old. Indeed, Winston Churchill later confessed that the U-boat menace was the most serious problem he faced throughout the war.

For the first fourteen months of America's entry into World War II, dedicated antisubmarine squadrons were exclusively land-based. Though spread wide on both sides of that contested ocean, their range left wide gaps in the trade routes where U-boats could operate with little fear of air attack.

Once Germany declared war on America, Admiral Karl Doenitz lost little time. In January 1942, the U-boat master sent wolfpacks to American waters, where they found perhaps the best hunting of the war. Ill-prepared for hostilities, the Atlantic coast continued to glow with city lights and navigation beacons operating normally. The U-boat crews could hardly believe their good fortune and sent twenty-six ships to the bottom off the US and Canadian coasts that month. In February, U-boats

F4F Wildcats and England-bound lend lease Martlet Is are mixed with J4F Widgeons at Grumman's Bethpage facility awaiting delivery. With the advent of war, US aircraft production skyrocketed bringing a US Navy and Marine Corps total of 4,196 heavier-than-air aircraft on 1 Jul 1939 to 14,116 by mid-1942. *Grumman*

VGS-27 Grumman F4F-3 Wildcat "Rosenblatt's Reply," is prepared for launch from *Suwanee* (ACV-27). Appearance of repainting over yellow surround of national insignia indicates photo was taken after Operation Torch in late 1942 or early 1943. *US Navy/ENS Barrett Gallagher*

slipped into the Gulf of Mexico, preying on oil-laden tankers and assorted merchantmen. Forty-two sinkings were recorded, as tonnage scores climbed and more Knights' Crosses were awarded sub skippers. Student naval aviators flying out of Corpus Christi, Texas, found miles of beaches polluted with oil from sunken ships.

The situation did not markedly improve, as throughout 1942 Allied shipping losses continued to exceed new construction. However, measures were taken which would slowly alleviate the crisis.

Elements of the Neutrality Patrol were already positioned when the shooting war started. Patrol Wing Seven covered the northern routes from Newfoundland and Iceland. Patrol Wing Five operated out of Norfolk, Virginia, and Patrol Wing Three flew from the Panama Canal Zone. Natal, Brazil, had been prepared as an ASW base in December 1941, and by late 1942 three patrol squadrons were operational there. Eventually they were joined by Martin PBM Mariners and Lockheed PV Venturas of Fleet Air Wing 16 in 1943.

Meanwhile, the German submarine force continued to enjoy fine hunting in American waters. The enemy crews termed this period "The second happy time," for only once before had they racked up such fat scores. May 1942 was the worst month yet, with seventy-two sinkings. While few submarines were lost, the VP squadrons did score occasional successes. That summer a VP-73 Catalina made a direct hit, impaling a depth charge in the wooden planking of a surfaced U-boat. A courageous, if unenlightened, crewman lifted the bomb out and pushed it overboard. The PBY crew watched incredulously as the depth charge reached its preset depth and exploded under the sub. A confirmed kill.

Gradually the ASW squadrons assimilated their experience and evolved a workable doctrine. New equipment also helped, as improved search radar, more effective weapons, and more efficient aircraft arrived. The submarine war was perhaps the most technological of all, and small improvements in detection or warning equipment gave each side temporary advantages in the see-saw contest.

Perhaps best-suited for the ASW role was Consolidated's big four-engine Liberator bomber. Designed for the Army Air Corps as the B-24, the Liberator became the PB4Y-1 in Navy service, later modified to the Privateer in the single-tail PB4Y-2 model. With exceptional range and armament capacity, it made an excellent sub hunter. But so did aircraft as different as the PBM Mariner flying boat and the slow, underrated blimp.

The Navy had operated both rigid and nonrigid airships well before World War II. But dirigibles had departed the scene during the 1930s, leaving only nonrigid (frameless) airships, or blimps, also known as "poopy bags" by the irreverent.

Origin of the word "blimp" is generically contested and widely ignored among heavier-than-air devotees. It is sometimes accredited to the sound made when one's finger is flipped against one of the inflated bags. What is known, however, is that Congress authorized an increase in Navy blimp strength to 200 airships in June 1942.

Three types of blimps were employed by the Navy during the war. The most common was the K-ship, which largely replaced the smaller L-type. ZPKs (lighter-than-air patrol type K) were 250ft long with 400,000 cubic feet of helium capacity. Intended primarily as ASW platforms, they carried radar, sonobuoys, and depth charges in addition to a new gadget, the magnetic anomaly detector (MAD). MAD had the advantage of being a passive underwater detector but had to be used at very low altitudes, usually below 200ft.

Larger M-ships were produced during the war but failed to replace the K series. Their advantages in relation to cost were too limited to warrant large-scale production.

In May 1943, the vice chief of Naval Operations approved ten LTA sites on the Brazilian coast to expand convoy protection. A major base was established near Rio de Janeiro, the Santa Cruz facility with its giant shed which previously serviced Germany's showpiece, the *Graf Zeppelin*. The Santa Cruz base would prove capable of operating and maintaining a dozen airships. By September, Fleet Airship Wing Four had begun operations, conducting convoy patrol and rescue work.

The rescue role afforded by blimps caught the Coast Guard's interest in the era before practical helicopters. Experiments conducted by the USCG Air-Sea Rescue Service found that raft-to-blimp transfers were possible, thereby expanding the realm of maritime lifesaving. The Coast Guardsmen urged adoption of the technique as standard practice, and while apparently few rescues were performed, the concept was well proven.

Meanwhile, Gulf Coast "BlimpRons" had been established. Aggressive U-boat sorties into the Gulf of Mexico required several LTA stations, each capable of handling as many as six ships. Inevitably built on marshes, these facilities featured large, hungry mosquitos and ever-present mud.

While the mere presence of aircraft could keep submarines submerged and therefore out of range of convoys, the Germans proved willing to surface and fight on several occasions. In one of the more bizarre combats of World War II, ship

Grumman/Eastern Aircraft FM-2 Wildcat pilots train aboard *Charger* (CVE-30) in Chesapeake Bay. Aircraft are in the Atlantic theater gray/white ASW camouflage scheme. *Charger* served the war as a training and developmental carrier for Atlantic Fleet units. *US Navy*

VF-1 (changed to VF-5 15 Jul 43) Grumman F6F-3 Hellcat over the ramp for recovery aboard *Yorktown* (CV-10) during her May–June 1943 shakedown off Trinidad. Hellcat production began in 1942 and initial fleet deliveries were to VF-9, scheduled for an early 1943 deployment to the Pacific. *US Navy/LT Charles Kerlee, courtesy Don S. Montgomery*

K-74 of Florida-based ZP-21 engaged *U-134* in a blimp-submarine shootout. It was not much of a contest, as blimps were intended to stalk submerged U-boats. With heavy-caliber automatic weapons, a surfaced submarine could shred a blimp's envelope in seconds. One crewman was lost in the action.

Though not an Atlantic Fleet event, the most bizarre episode in World War II blimp lore involved a ship that returned without its crew. In August 1942, ZP-32's *L-8* took off from Treasure Island in San Francisco Bay. Early that morning the two-man crew, both officers, reported an oil slick, saying they were investigating. Nothing more was heard of them.

Almost four hours later, *L-8* alit in Daly City, having scraped off a depth charge on a nearby hill. Neither Ensign C.E. Adams nor Lieutenant (jg) E.D. Cody were aboard. The mystery of their disappearance remains unsolved more than half a century later.

During early 1944, ten ASW BlimpRons were organized as Fleet Airships Atlantic under Commodore G.H. Mills. They stretched from Nova Scotia to Rio de Janeiro, providing Atlantic coast convoy protection the length of the New World. But blimps would operate on the far side of the ocean as well.

Commander E.J. Sullivan's ZP-14 was based in North Carolina when chosen to fly to Africa. The unit prepared its staging base at NAS South Weymouth, Massachussetts, and dispatched the first pair of ships, *K-123* and *-130*, on 28 May 1944. Following the Newfoundland-Azores route, the two blimps arrived at Port Lyautey, French Morocco, on 1 June, after a fifty-eight-hour transit. It was the first Atlantic crossing by nonrigid airships, but not the last.

Another ASW innovation was establishment, in 1942, of fifteen inshore patrol squadrons in the East Coast and Caribbean. These squadrons guarded America's Atlantic shoreline and navigable waterways, as U-boats even were reported in Chesapeake Bay. Assigned to the various Sea Frontiers, the inshore squadrons originally carried designations related to the naval districts where they were based. For instance, VS-1D5 was Scouting Squadron One, Fifth Naval District.

Fifteen similar units were established on the West Coast, at Coco Solo and Pearl Harbor. On 17 October 1942, the inshore patrol squadrons came under administrative control of the

continued on page 42

Right
During WWII, the Naval Air Modification Unit (NAMU), located at Johnsville, Pa., was a division of the Naval Air Material Center, Philadelphia, responsible for development of modification programs for naval aircraft. This F6F-3K Hellcat was part of a drone development program at NAMU during August 1945. Yellow paint scheme was used at the time for utility, drone, and training aircraft. *NASM*

Below
Douglas XJD-1 BuNo 57991 assigned to VJ-4 at NAS Norfolk, 13 Jul 1945, was the second of two USAAF A-26B Invaders to be adapted for use in US Navy utility work. A total of 140 A-26Cs were acquired for Navy use as JD-1s (UB-26J) and JD-1Ds (DB-26J) drone control aircraft. *US Navy, courtesy Dick Starinchak*

Left
Fleet Air Photographic Squadron Atlantic Grumman J2F-2A Duck crew practices an at-sea rescue mission off the East Coast c. 1942–43. Nine J2F-2s were modified in 1939 with machine guns and bomb racks for use with VMS-3 in the Virgin Islands as part of the neutrality patrol. *US Navy*

Below
Radioman-gunner of one of Operation Torch's SBD-3 squadrons, exercises his twin-.30 cal. machine guns as a squadron ordnanceman (with helmet) and another aircrewman observe. SBD crews flew from four carriers in support of the North African invasion 8–13 Nov 1942. *US Navy, courtesy Russ Egnor*

continued from page 39

patrol wings. On 1 March 1943 they were redesignated normal VS (scouting) squadrons.

Originally flying Vought OS2U Kingfishers, the squadrons also acquired Douglas SBDs for their ASW mission. By mid-1944, with the U-boat threat greatly diminished, the inshore patrol squadrons began disbanding. By war's end, they were gone.

New bases helped close the "Atlantic Gap" where air coverage previously had never existed. Airfields in the West Indies, the Brazilian coast, then Ascension Island did much to expand convoy protection.

But new aircraft and improved gadgets could not alone defeat the aggressive wolfpacks. When merchant sinkings began to trail off that fall of 1942, it was as much the result of perseverance as anything. Persistence counted for a great deal in antisubmarine warfare: the willingness to stick with a contact, cap a sub in relays if necessary until it had no choice but to surface. As Fleet Air Wing 16 noted, "It has been a war where patience and steadiness have counted for as much as brilliance and dash in other theaters where there has been more shooting."

JRF-5 Goose is readied for flight at Grumman's Bethpage, New York, facility during July-August 1942. The -5 was the main production model of the utility transport. *NASM courtesy, Jeff Ethell*

February 1943 photo of a VJ-4 Sikorsky JRS-1 amphibian at NAS Miami. Seventeen JRS-1s were purchased for use by USN/USMC utility squadrons. *US Navy, courtesy Stan Piet*

Despite the immense drain on naval aviation resources to fight the Battle of the Atlantic, other plans were proceeding in the winter of 1942. Consequently, *Ranger* embarked her air group and began workups for the most ambitious naval operation yet conducted in the European-African area. Simultaneous Anglo-American amphibious landings were scheduled for Morocco and Algeria in early November 1942: Operation Torch.

Supporting the American effort were four carriers operating in three task groups. Their combined strength numbered 62 bombers (Douglas SBD-3 Dauntlesses and Grumman TBF-1 Avengers) plus 109 F4F-4s. Battleship- and cruiser-based floatplanes also contributed scout-observation and rescue capability to the task force.

The US landings were centered upon Casablanca, with additional beaches to the north and south. *Ranger* and the escort carrier *Suwanee* (ACV-27) steamed off Casablanca, while *Sangamon* (ACV-26) and *Santee* (ACV-29) operated off the northern and southern areas, respectively. Escort carriers—originally "auxiliary aircraft carriers"—subsequently were redesignated CVEs on 15 July 1943.

The overall aviator experience level was low; average flight time in one fighting squadron amounted to a mere 400 hours. However, VF-4 in *Ranger* had been the original Wildcat unit, and Lieutenant Commander C.T. Booth's pilots generally had 500 or more hours in F4Fs alone. But the task force had been assembled and dispatched so fast that there had been

almost no opportunity to practice, and some pilots had not flown in two weeks.

The major question, however, was not the fliers' experience, but enemy reaction. Morocco was garrisoned by Vichy forces, technically guarding unoccupied French territory from invasion. Opinion was divided as to whether or not the Vichy forces would oppose the American landings; there was no doubt they would fight the British.

French Navy and Air Force squadrons amounted to almost 200 planes, including numerous American-built Martin and Douglas bombers and Curtiss fighters. Many of the Vichy pilots were combat veterans of the Battle of France, now obliged to fight the very men who had come to begin the liberation of France. For further irony, one of the French fighter units traced

Close-up view of a Douglas SBD-4 gunner from VC-22 assigned to *Independence* (CV-22) 30 Apr 1943. On 15 Jul 1943, the Independence-class light carriers (built on cruiser hulls) were reclassified CVL. Photo well describes typical flight gear, armor plate, and red-tipped tracer rounds of the period. *US Navy, courtesy Russ Egnor*

During her October 1943 shakedown in the Atlantic, *Biloxi* (CL-80) carried Curtiss SO3C-1 Seamews. Scheduled to replace the "obsolete" SOC, the SO3Cs failed to perform satisfactorily and were withdrawn in 1944, while the SOCs were reactivated. *US Navy, courtesy Russ Egnor*

its ancestry to the *Escadrille Lafayette*, the squadron of American volunteer pilots in World War I.

The landings began at dawn on 8 November. But in hope of avoiding conflict, American aviators were forbidden to shoot unless fired upon. The radio call sign for French opposition was "Batter up." The task force would then authorize return fire by calling "Play ball."

The game began poorly. A flight of seven *Santee* fighters became disoriented and ran low on fuel. One ditched at sea and five crash-landed ashore. Though these six pilots turned up safe, another had disappeared and was later reported killed.

Ranger's VF-4 and VF-9 learned the hard way that they could not dogfight the agile French fighters and learned to respect automatic weapons fire from the ground. Fighting Four lost six Wildcats in its first mission, though VF-26 from *Sangamon* claimed three bombers and a fighter without loss.

However, the center of attraction in Casablanca Harbor was the French battleship *Jean Bart*, adding her 15 inch guns to the shore batteries. Eighteen *Ranger* scout-bombers attacked naval facilities in the harbor, including submarine moorings and *Jean Bart* herself. The battleship was hit, though not fatally, while one submarine was sunk.

The ubiquitous Piper Cub got into the war in naval service as AE, HE and NE versions nicknamed Grasshopper. They were primarily used at elimination bases or as utility and hospital evacuation planes at air stations around the country. NE-1 BuNo 25381 was assigned to NAS Norfolk in 1942. *US Navy, courtesy Doug Siegfried*

When a French cruiser-destroyer force sortied to engage the American warships, SBDs and F4Fs dropped down to bomb and strafe. A light cruiser and two destroyers were beached to prevent their sinking.

The secondary objectives, Fedala to the north and Safi to the south, were captured during the first day. Port Lyautey was taken the following afternoon, with P-40s being flown ashore from *Chenango* (ACV-28).

Meanwhile, SBDs and TBFs flew antisubmarine patrol and attacked enemy airfields and strongpoints. But Casablanca's batteries continued to give trouble until 9 November. Nine of *Ranger's* Dauntlesses attacked with 1,000 pound bombs, scoring two direct hits, which finally put *Jean Bart* out of action. The French surrender came early on the morning of 11 November—twenty-four years to the day after the end of "the war to end all wars."

A Skipper's Story

T. Hugh Winters was a Navy junior who grew up in the service and graduated from Annapolis in 1935. As a prewar aviator, he brought invaluable experience to VF-9, filled out with "nugget" pilots new to the fleet when beginning combat operations off Morocco.

Before entrusting command of a newly forming squadron to an apparently qualified pilot, the Navy works him over pretty thoroughly, and it is more than a college cram course. After eyeballing his record for several years back, they put him through some sort of obstacle course such as I went through to qualify for command.

First, two years as a dive bomber pilot in the old York-town, a most valuable experience for a future fighter pilot. Then, exec of a new fighting squadron (VF-9) under an experienced skipper, Jack Raby. I knew how to fly and how to shoot; Jack taught me the value of comradeship to a unit, the loyalty engendered by squadron parties, squadron outings of every sort includ-

The Coast Guard acquired seven Hall PH-3s in 1939 which were used until 1944 for ASW patrols. Nose gunner test fires his .30 cal. machine gun during a 1942 patrol mission. *US Navy, courtesy Jeff Ethell*

NAS Norfolk, Va., was an important patrol plane base throughout the war, utilized for both training and ASW missions. Martin PBM-3 Mariner is launched at a Norfolk seaplane ramp c. 1942–43. *US Navy, courtesy Stan Piet*

A VR-6 Martin PBM-3R Mariner bobs on its mooring lines at NAS Banana River c. 1943. *US Navy*

VP-31 Consolidated PBY-5A Catalina at NAS Norfolk, Va., c. 1942-43. PBYs of VP-63 were the first magnetic anomaly detection-equipped (MAD) aircraft in Europe, reporting to the U.K. in July 1943. *US Navy, courtesy Stan Piet*

NAS Norfolk beaching crew launches a VP-51 Consolidated PBY-5 Catalina into Willoughby Bay. Placement of the national insignia on the nose indicates the "Cat" is assigned to the neutrality patrol. VP-51 began receiving -5s during April 1941. *US Navy, courtesy Jeff Ethell*

A contract for production of Grumman's TBF-1 Avenger was let even before the first flight of the XTBF-1. VT-8 was the first squadron to receive the new torpedo bomber, taking delivery of its first aircraft 25 May 1942. The squadron operated as a split unit partly at NAS Norfolk while its operational TBD-1s and aircrew were embarked in *Hornet* (CV-8). The latter were already en route to the Battle of Midway and annihilation. Six VT-8 Avengers made it to Midway, but only one returned, flown by ENS Bert Earnest, with a dead gunner and wounded radioman. Publicity photo shows VT-8 crew manning a new TBF-1. Original four-man crew was reduced by eliminating the horizontal bombardier behind the pilot. *Rudy Arnold, courtesy Lois Lovisolo*

ing, of course, all the wives and girlfriends. It was a truism in Jack's squadron that when any member thought of a social event he thought squadron event: birthdays, weddings, the whole bit. Since all of our boys were from far away, the squadron brought them very close together and it was, for the time being, their life.

The exec does a great deal of the work in forming and training a new squadron, and then goes with it into combat. This allows the skipper to concern himself with major decisions, not getting too engrossed in details, and also to argue with the staff for better treatment of his outfit. Jack was very good at all these and gave me free rein in air tactics and gunnery training, and together we developed some of the finest fighter gunners of the war: Gene Valencia, Ham McWhorter, Marv Franger, Mike Hadden, Lou Menard, Chick Smith, Hal Vita, and several other aces.

We cut our teeth in combat over North Africa in November 1942, knocking out Vichy French aircraft threatening Mark Clark's assault in the Port Lyautey-Casablanca area in a hectic three-day battle. We had been squeezed into the Ranger along with her own VF-41 to ensure air superiority over that part of Morocco.

I averaged three missions a day, and actually felt safer in the air than on the ship, as the antique gasoline system leaked so badly you could sometimes smell high-test gas. The U-boats were all around us. One day our landing signal officer, Bunky Ottinger, waved off two torpedoes passing under the fantail and had witnesses to prove it!

We had three tragic losses in this action, and I had to watch two of them. The first was my wingman, Willie Wilhoite,

Douglas SBD-3 Dauntlesses of VGS-26 and Grumman F4F-4 Wildcats of VGF-26 are spotted tightly on *Sangamon's* (ACV-26) flight deck during Operation Torch, the invasion of North Africa in November 1942. Distance and other target information for her aircrews is chalked on deck. *US Navy, Russ Egnor*

who had flown with me all summer. We were strafing fighters on the Port Lyautey field and I had just exploded a gas truck between two fighters refueling, and pulling out I heard Willie call, "They got me, Pedro." He glided steeply into the ground about a mile from the field. I did a wingover and went back at ground level on the machine-gun nest and got hit myself, but not seriously. Expensive lesson learned—never in the heat of rage do a wingover at close range.

Next day we were burning some bombers on another field and Eddie Micha exploded one with bombs attached just as he passed over it at 20 feet altitude. The blast converted his little Wildcat into a large ball of fire bouncing along the run-way. The loss of Willie, and then right away Eddie, added some to my 29 years.

Winters was preparing to assume command of Fighting Nine when he was detached to establish VF-19. Deployed to the Western Pacific, he became *Lexington's* air group commander during the second half of 1944.

Aside from outflanking the Axis forces in North Africa, Operation Torch provided naval aviators with a relatively mild introduction to combat. Air-ground support tactics had been proven, and antisubmarine techniques tested. *Suwanee's* Avengers, in fact, sank at least one French boat at sea.

In aerial combat the untried F4F pilots downed about five opponents for each loss, having learned early that mutual support and maintaining airspeed led to success. But carrier aircraft losses to ground fire and operational causes were steep.

With nearly 25 percent aircraft attrition in three days, the task force could not have sustained operations much longer. That, too, was a lesson learned.

After Torch, naval aviation in the Atlantic focused increasingly upon antisubmarine warfare (ASW). Fleet Air Wing Fifteen's two original squadrons were flying from Casablanca and Port Lyautey within hours of the French surrender on Armistice Day 1942, and they were badly needed. Axis submarines sank eleven Allied ships and damaged five more during Torch itself; the toll only increased.

Ventura and Liberator squadrons added their weight to the ubiquitous PBYs during early 1943, covering the North Atlantic trade routes from Iceland to Morocco, to the extent of their range. Meanwhile, a permanent institution for studying aerial ASW was established at Quonset Point, Rhode Island. The Antisubmarine Development Detachment conducted operational research into the best methods of combating the resourceful, elusive U-boat.

But the Germans had new ideas themselves. As Allied coastal patrols increased, Luftwaffe maritime aircraft became increasingly aggressive during May 1943. Previously, Focke-Wulf 200s and other long-range aircraft had been mainly content to shadow convoys, reporting their position, course, and speed. Now the German *seeflieger* attacked ships more frequently in the

Hornet (CV-8), with her Grumman F4F-3 Wildcats of VF-8 on deck, is moored at Norfolk in February 1942, just prior to her transfer to the Pacific Fleet the following month. In April, she would launch the famous Doolittle Raid B-25s against Tokyo. *US Navy*

Below
VCS-10 Vought OS2U-3 Kingfisher is fired from *Quincy's* (CA-71) catapult during Atlantic operations c. 1944. *Quincy's* OS2Us provided air spotting for shore bombardment of German mobile batteries, as well as tank, truck and troop concentrations during the Normandy invasion 6-17 Jun 1944. *US Navy*

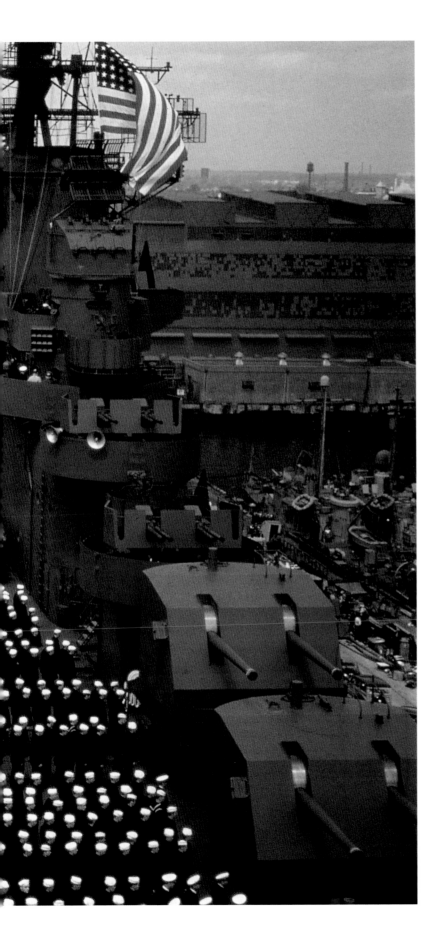

Sangamon (ACV-26) steams with her escort *Hamilton* (DD-455) en route to Operation Torch, the invasion of North Africa, during November 1942. Escort carriers were originally classified AVGs (Aircraft Escort Vessels), then changed to ACVs (Auxiliary Aircraft Carriers) 20 Aug 1942 and finally to CVE (Escort Aircraft Carriers) 15 Jul 1943. *US Navy, courtesy Stan Piet*

Left
Following *Yorktown's* (CV-5) loss at Midway in June 1942, a new *Yorktown* (CV-10) was commissioned 15 Apr 1943 at Newport News Shipbuilding Co. The second of the 24 magnificent Essex-class carriers to be constructed, CV-10 became known as "The Fighting Lady" and is now preserved as a museum at Charleston, S.C. All Fast Carriers of WWII, as well as the follow-on Midway-class and later supercarriers, were built on the East Coast. *US Navy, courtesy Don S. Montgomery*

Bay of Biscay, diverting Allied squadrons from ASW work to convoy air defense.

That summer Doenitz ordered his U-boat skippers to stand up to aircraft, remaining surfaced to shoot it out. The "fight back" tactic resulted in casualties on both sides. For instance, FAW-15 out of Gibraltar made sixteen attacks on submarines during the first half of June, claiming five kills. But three Liberators and a Catalina were badly damaged by return fire.

Bay of Biscay flights now regularly met aggressive Junkers 88s, and Luftwaffe aircraft contested the Mediterranean approaches as well. Perhaps the most bizarre aerial combat of the war occurred on 12 June as two Condors fought two PBYs assigned to cover a rescue ship en route to Casablanca. One Catalina stayed low to watch for reported submarines, but the other could not climb fast enough to prevent an attack on the ship, which sustained a bomb hit.

Lexington (CV-16) is launched at Fall River, Mass., 29 Sep 1942. Commissioned 17 Feb 1943, she would be the longest lived of the Essexes, serving as an attack carrier during the '50s and as a training carrier until 8 Nov 1991. *US Navy, courtesy Stan Piet*

As the Condors closed for the kill, the remaining PBY met them head-on time after time. Though considerable ammunition was expended on both sides, the ship was saved by the P-boat pilot's determination to force the Germans off course during their attacks.

Meanwhile, Fleet Air Wing Seven had established itself at Dunkeswell, Devon, as the resident US Navy ASW unit in Britain. In late July 1943, VP-63 (a PBY squadron) joined the PB4Ys of VP-103 and -105. Equipped with magnetic anomaly gear, PatRon 63's Catalinas became the first "MAD Cats" in the U.K. But their tour began poorly, losing a plane to German fighters on the second day of operations. It fit the pattern, for another FAW-7 unit, VB-110, lost half its PB4Ys and one-third of its crews in the first six months. Weather and enemy aircraft were factors to be reckoned with.

The first U-boat kill by a MAD-equipped aircraft was on 24 February 1944, when VP-63, two other squadrons, and two ships joined forces to sink *U-76* in the Strait of Gibraltar.

However, August 1943 was a banner month, with only two merchantmen sunk in areas patrolled by US Navy aircraft. There were no submarine kills in September, but FAW-7 was busy anyway. Increasing German fighter patrols in the Bay of Biscay forced the Liberators to practice air-to-air combat tactics. The wing doctrine was primarily evasion, turning to a westerly heading at first sign of interceptors. But the situation was reminiscent of heavyweight boxing champ Joe Louis' wisdom: "You can run but you can't hide." The faster German aircraft usually could overtake a PB4Y and force a combat. Ju-88s and twin-engine Messerschmitts downed two Liberators that month and two more in October. Since the Libs seldom flew anything but solo patrols, they were vastly outnumbered by enemy formations of six or more aircraft.

Ordered as a back-up program for the TBF, Vought was to produce the TBU Seawolf as a Navy torpedo bomber. Because of Vought's heavy F4U commitments, the Seawolf production contract was given to Consolidated-Vultee in September 1943. The company produced 180 TBY-2s, but the airplane became operational with only one squadron, VT-154 at NAS Quonset Point, R.I., late in the war. *Courtesy Rae Klahr*

Above
Fleet Air Wing Seven operated Consolidated PB4Y-1 Liberators from Dunkeswell, Devon, U.K. FAW-7 had three PB4Y squadrons—VP-103, -105 and -110. The latter squadron fared poorly in the beginning as it lost half its aircraft and one-third of its crews in the first six months of European operations. *US Navy*

Right
Grumman TBF-1 Avenger in flight c. 1942. Unable to meet the heavy production requirements of WWII for its TBF, F4F, and F6F tactical aircraft, the Avenger and Wildcat were also built by Eastern Aircraft Division of General Motors as TBMs and FMs. A total of 9,836 Avengers was built by both companies for the US Navy as well as Allied countries. *Grumman, courtesy H.L. Schonenberg*

Nor were Germans the only threat, as FAW-15 planes were harassed by Spanish fighters. On at least one occasion a PBY was attacked and narrowly escaped. The air wing staff had a remedy for that. Two speedy, well-armed Lockheed PV Venturas were deployed to Agadir, Morocco, and took over the PBY patrol route. The next time the "neutral" Spaniards came up to play, they found more sport than anticipated. The potent PV foiled any subsequent mischief, without loss to either party.

Operating under RAF Coastal Command, Air Wing Seven played an important role in the D-Day landings in Normandy. Dawn-to-dusk patrols kept the Germans at bay and no Allied ships were lost to U-boats in the ensuing three weeks. During that period the Liberators made seventeen attacks, leading to some dandy shootouts, but there were no aircraft losses.

A postscript to the Dunkeswell story involved equal portions of technical innovation and tragedy. Lieutenant Joseph P. Kennedy, Jr., was the son of the former American ambassador to the U.K., who had resigned in 1940, convinced that Germany would win the war. As a patrol-plane commander in VB-110, young Joe completed some fifty missions from mid-1943 to the summer of 1944. Squadronmates recall him as "one hell of an aviator" who sometimes exhibited "more guts than good sense." On one occasion when his lone PB4Y was jumped by two Messerschmitt 210 fighters, Kennedy ignored doctrine and turned into the attack so his gunner could open fire. The Messerschmitts disengaged.

Kennedy was recruited for Project Aphrodite, a joint program with the Army Air Forces which began in June 1944. It involved loading war-weary bombers with tons of high explosives and guiding them to precision targets by remote control. State-of-the-art technology did not permit the drones to take off without a pilot and ordnanceman aboard to arm the explosives. Once under remote control from the PV-1 lead ship, the two-man crew bailed out and the mission proceeded.

Kennedy and his copilot, Lieutenant W.J. Willey, were assigned a PB4Y-1 called *Zoot Suit Black*. Their Liberator was loaded with 12 tons of Torpex intended for a V-1 missile site in northern France. They took off safely on 12 August and headed for the Suffolk coast when *Zoot Suit Black* exploded for no apparent reason. Both men died instantly. The effect upon history was that Joe's younger brother John—a wartime PT-boat skipper—became president of the United States in 1960.

While Aphrodite missions did hit some difficult targets such as rocket sites, the overall project was a marginal success. Advancing technology would be required before such "smart bombs" reached a degree of reliability. But dedicated aviators like Kennedy and Willey had helped show the way.

ASW paint scheme-clad Grumman TBF-1 Avenger "in the groove" for landing aboard *Charger* (CVE-30) 22 Apr 1944. *Charger* operated throughout the war in Chesapeake Bay as a training and developmental carrier. *US Navy, courtesy Russ Egnor*

Left
America's aircraft manufacturers began gearing up for mass production even before the United States entered the war. Douglas SBD-5 Dauntless assembly line at El Segundo, Calif., c. July 1942. Horizontal bars and red surround were added to the national insignia in July 1943. The red paint was directed to be replaced by blue 31 Jul 1943 to avoid confusion with red Japanese Hinamaru insignia. All aircraft were not immediately repainted, especially those in the combat zone, and some carried the red markings for several months. *Douglas, courtesy Harry Gann*

Below
Aviation Ordnancemen boresight .50 cal. machine guns of Grumman F4F-4 Wildcat. F4F-4s differed from the -3 by having folding wings and six .50 cal. wing-mounted guns instead of four. *US Navy, courtesy Russ Egnor*

Curtiss' SB2C-1 Helldiver almost didn't make it into full operational service and wouldn't have if *Yorktown's* (CV-10) skipper CAPT J.J. "Jocko" Clark would have had his way. Because of inordinate structural problems, as seen with this SB2C tailwheel collapse on board CV-10, Clark recommended cancellation of the Helldiver contract. *US Navy/LT Charles Kerlee, courtesy Russ Egnor*

Another aspect of land-based naval aviation was involved in the D-Day period. Allied experience in the amphibious invasion of Sicily and Italy proved the extreme vulnerability of slow, lightly armed floatplanes to enemy fighters. But the VOS aircraft were needed to call naval gunfire. Therefore, the British equipped five RAF squadrons and four Fleet Air Arm units with single-seat fighters flown by specially trained pilots who could perform the spotting mission.

The US Navy followed suit. Seventeen pilots from the VOS units of the three American battleships and three cruisers assigned to Operation Overlord were pulled out for fighter training. Instruction by the Royal Navy at Lee-on-Solent,

Hampshire, got the Americans qualified in Supermarine Spitfires borrowed from the US Ninth Air Force. Then they learned standardized techniques that would allow them to work with any Allied ship on D-Day. Aside from the obvious benefit of greatly improved self-defense, the erstwhile floatplane pilots reveled in the thrill of flying one of the world's most glamorous fighters.

All ten naval support squadrons operated from Lee-on-Solent, not only spotting naval gunfire but flying tactical reconnaissance as well. The US Navy pilots flew 10 percent of all such sorties in the three weeks following D-Day, contributing their special skill and knowledge to the Allied effort.

Despite extended coverage by land-based aircraft, in early 1943 Allied convoys still sailed hundreds of miles of the Atlantic beyond air cover. The answer to the problem was obvious. The merchantmen needed to sail beneath their own air umbrella.

The solution was the escort carrier with specially equipped planes flown by aircrews trained for antisubmarine warfare. The first of these "baby flattops" were conversions from freighter hulls. And babies they were, compared with the new 27,100-ton Essex-class carriers. Most CVEs were less than 500 feet in length, displacing less than 15,000 tons fully loaded. They operated fewer than 30 planes and steamed at a maximum 17 to 19 knots.

With the grim humor common to sailors, escort-carrier crews said that CVE stood for "combustible, vulnerable, and expendable." Others described the little flattops as "two-torpedo ships." The second torpedo, they said, usually went over the flight deck.

Certainly the CVEs were not much compared with the eighty-plane air groups of the upcoming Essexes, with their top speeds of more than 30 knots. But the CVEs were well suited to their specialized role. They could easily keep pace with merchant convoys, and their planes had only one task: hunting submarines—and killing them.

Grumman F4F-3 Wildcat wears the two-tone, blue-gray and light gray scheme in effect during late 1941 through 1942. Red horizontal rudder stripes were used January–May 1942. Enlarged national insignia was used by some units on both the fuselage and wings during 1942. All red markings were ordered removed in May 1942. *Rudy Arnold, courtesy H.L. Schonenberg*

rific amounts of flak from German submarines. Multiple-mount 20- and 37mm antiaircraft guns made surfaced U-boats formidable opponents, and Doenitz's "fight-back" tactics were widely employed.

The peril to airmen was demonstrated on 13 July. An Avenger and Wildcat of *Core's* VC-13 caught the tanker *U-487* (the Germans often used submarine tankers to replenish their wolfpacks at sea) and, according to doctrine, split to divide the defenses. But the German gunners shot down the fighter and kept the TBF at bay. Finally, three more planes were called in before another Avenger could finish the job.

Obviously, the battle was heating up. But *Santee* aircraft destroyed two U-boats without difficulty during the next two days. When the U-boats submerged, TBFs were on hand with the new Fido homing torpedoes which faithfully followed their targets' engine noise.

With six kills during July and six more in August, the U-boat war had taken a decided turn for the better from the carrier airmens' viewpoint, to say nothing of the merchant sailors. Things thinned out during the fall months, but by the end of the year, CVEs had destroyed 23 U-boats in seven months. CompRon Nine, flying first from *Bogue* and then from *Card* (CVE-11), was responsible for eight kills.

The next power-projection mission for an American carrier in European waters occurred almost a year after Torch. Again, *Ranger* was involved. Operating with the British Home Fleet, she was alerted for an unusual mission: Operation Leader, a strike against Axis shipping in and around Bodo Harbor on the Norwegian coast.

Ranger reached launch position about dawn on 3 October 1943, escorted by a powerful British force. The carrier put up two strikes: 20 Dauntlesses followed by 10 Avengers, each escorted by six to eight Wildcats. Making a low-level approach to avoid radar detection, each wave climbed to attack altitude within visible distance of the rocky shore. Then, in succession, the bombers went after coastal targets of opportunity and shipping anchored in the harbor.

There was no airborne opposition, though a four-plane division of CAP Wildcats splashed two German reconnaissance aircraft near the task force. Between them, VB-4 and VT-4 destroyed six ships and seriously damaged three more. Three bombers were lost, and one fighter was extensively damaged. Undeniably successful, Operation Leader marked the end of *Ranger's* combat career. She would soon report to the West Coast of the United States, serving as a training carrier for the remainder of the war.

VOF-1 F6F-5 pilot takes a waveoff from LSO during a landing attempt aboard *Tulagi* (CVE-72), following an air-support mission over Southern France on D-Day for Operation Dragoon invasion 15 Aug 1944. *US Navy, courtesy Russ Egnor*

By the spring of 1944, some of the ASW excitement had abated. Contacts were less frequent, and aircrews flew hours and hours along the convoy routes without a sighting. In fact, the hunter-killers bagged only nine U-boats in the Atlantic through-

Section of factory-fresh F6F-3 Hellcats off the East Coast during summer 1943. The formidable Grumman fighter earned its fame in the Pacific but also served vital roles in the Atlantic on a smaller scale. *Grumman, courtesy H.L. Schonenberg*

out the year. But the reduced pace of combat by no means eliminated all the excitement, or casualties. On two occasions TBFs pressed their attacks so close that they were destroyed by the explosion of their own bombs.

Nor were the losses limited to airplanes and flight crews. On 29 May a U-boat torpedoed *Block Island* (CVE-21)

off the African coast. She was the only US carrier sunk in the Atlantic, and she was immediately avenged by the destroyers of her screen. In four ASW cruises her planes had sunk two U-boats and assisted in two more kills. During January one of her Avengers had made the first American rocket attack on a submarine.

Sikorsky HNS-1 Hoverfly and Goodyear K-ship blimp observe German *U-858* type IXC submarine being brought to anchor at Cape Henlopen, Del., in May 1945 after surrender at sea. Combined US naval aviation and British forces broke the back of the German U-boat campaign. During April and May 1943 50 U-boats were destroyed in the Atlantic and Bay of Biscay—26 by land-based aircraft and four by CVE aircraft. Most of those kills were by British forces, but US HUK (Hunter-Killer) groups accounted for 50 more U-boats by the end of the year. *US Navy, courtesy Russ Egnor*

Earlier that year the CVEs had begun experimenting with a means of harassing U-boats around the clock. Some of *Card's* TBMs were stripped of almost every possible pound to optimize fuel load. Even armament was sacrificed in an effort to gain maximum endurance. Reduced to a two-man crew of pilot and radarman, the modified Avengers could remain airborne as long as fourteen hours—more than enough to pursue a submarine contact from dusk to dawn. The aircraft could then call in destroyers to prosecute the contact.

Card's nocturnal fliers found no U-boats, but the next month, March 1944, brought substantial gains. CompRon 58 in *Guadalcanal* (CVE-60) began similar experiments, but Captain Daniel V. Gallery wanted his "night owls" to keep their talons. Once his Avenger pilots were night qualified, Gallery's staff worked out a relay schedule intended to maintain four TBMs airborne through the night. With preliminaries settled, VC-58 began nocturnal flying in earnest on 7 April.

The results were dramatic. During a thirty-day period of daylight operations, *Guadalcanal* had recorded not even a sighting. On the second and third nights of the new program, VC-58 shared one kill with destroyers and made a solo kill as well.

"Cap'n Dan" Gallery's hunter-killers figured prominently in an even more spectacular episode in early June. On the fourth—two days before the Normandy landings—VC-58 Wildcats found a submerged submarine. The fighters directed a destroyer-escort (DE) to the scene, which forced *U-505* to the surface. The Germans set scuttling charges and abandoned ship, but boats from the carrier and a DE put sailors aboard who disarmed the charges and kept the sub afloat.

Gallery had planned for such a contingency, and his foresight made him the only American U-boat hunter who added a "tame" seawolf to his trophy collection. It was the first time the US Navy had seized an enemy man-of-war on the high seas since sloop *Peacock* captured the British armed brig *Nautilus* in 1815.

Ignominiously, the German submarine was towed into Bermuda on 19 June, flying the stars and stripes. For the rest of his life, *Guadalcanal's* landing signal officer—Lieutenant "Stretch" Jennings—bragged that he was the only LSO ever to recover planes while towing a submarine.

Another unusual hunt was concluded late that month in the same area when *Bogue* aircraft tracked a submarine through the night of the 23rd. Expert sonobuoy use by VC-69 led to a confirmed kill of a Japanese boat, the big *I-52*. She had been on a liaison cruise to France, but never arrived. It was the only aerial kill of a Japanese submarine in the Atlantic Ocean.

Bogue, which had scored the first hunter-killer success, also recorded the last. That came on 20 August when several of her Avengers ganged up on *U-1229*. It was the thirty-first destruction of an enemy submarine by hunter-killer aircraft in the Atlantic. Allied ASW forces sank 791 U-boats during the war: two-thirds of those operational throughout the war. That U-boat morale held up to the last days was testimony to the superior leadership of Admiral Doenitz and his command. But no military force can sustain 85 percent personnel casualties and remain effective. Obviously, the US Navy's CVEs had performed services out of proportion to their number. That task was proven every time an Allied convoy dropped anchor at its destination, delivering all the supplies originally loaded aboard.

The last offensive involving US carriers in Europe offered a startling contrast from Operation Leader. The scene shifted from north of the Arctic Circle to the sunny French Riv-

VJ-4 personnel prepare gunnery target sleeve for December 1943 tow mission by Martin JM-1 Marauder from NAS Norfolk, Va. The Navy acquired 225 JM-1s (USAAF AT-23B/B-26C) and 47 JM-2s (TB-26G) for USN/USMC utility use. *US Navy/LT Horace Bristol, courtesy Russ Egnor*

iera as two carriers supported Operation Anvil/Dragoon, the invasion of southern France.

Not only were the climate and ships different, so too were the aircraft. By August 1944 the escort carriers *Tulagi* (CVE-72) and *Kasaan Bay* (CVE-69) each flew a squadron of Grumman F6F-5 Hellcats. *Ranger* had requested F6F-3s for Operation Leader, but none were then available because of pressing need in the Pacific. Now, however, there were plenty of Hellcats to go around. Each ship operated 24 of the fighter-bombers.

Also unusual was the background of *Tulagi's* miniature "air group." Observation-Fighting Squadron One (VOF-1) had been selected and trained as a gunnery spotting unit. Originally equipped with Vought F4U-1s, the squadron was informed that Corsairs could not safely operate from carriers. That came as a surprise to Lieutenant Commander W.F. Bringle's pilots, who had qualified aboard ship with little difficulty. So VOF-1 went

An effort to supplement the Navy's transport capabilities with an aircraft made from materials other than aluminum, was the all-steel Budd RB-1 Conestoga program begun in 1942. With a load capacity no greater than Douglas' R4D Skytrain, the Conestoga was canceled after only 26 aircraft. BuNo 39294 was accepted by the Navy 3 May 1944 and was stricken 21 Oct after brief service with NATS at Patuxent River. *US Navy, courtesy Russ Egnor*

to war with Hellcats, as did Lieutenant Commander H.B. Bass' VF-74 in *Kasaan Bay*.

Operation Dragoon was supported by seven British CVEs, but the F6F's superior range resulted in the American squadrons conducting most of the deep inshore reconnaissance flights.

On D-Day, 15 August, the Hellcats flew more than 100 sorties, directing naval gunfire against German troop concentrations and supply routes. But in the following several days all manner of sorties were flown: bombing, strafing, rocketing, and armed reconnaissance. German aircraft were first encountered on 19 August, and that evening a section of two VOF-1 Hellcats shot down three Heinkel 111 bombers.

But there were losses. In two line periods totaling thirteen days, the American F6F squadrons lost eleven aircraft, including five on the 20th. Four pilots were killed, including Lieutenant Commander Bass, lost to flak.

However, the two squadrons had done their job and more; over 800 vehicles were credited as destroyed and 84 locomotives were wrecked. "Rail outs" and other communications cuts were also accomplished. The air-to-air score was computed at eight to nothing, as all the Hellcats' shootdowns were multi-engine Heinkels or Junkers.

Hellcats Over France

Hailing from St. Louis, Missouri, Ensign Edward W. Olszewski originally was trained as a dive bomber pilot. He was a plankowner when Observation-Fighting Squadron One was established in December 1943, and entered combat during the invasion of Southern France in August 1944.

On 21 August a flight of eight Hellcats led by Lieutenant Frederick "Sandy" Schauffler headed up the Rhone River Valley with myself in the number three spot and my wingman, Ensign Richard "Bub" Yentzer, in number four.

Vought's OS2U Kingfisher remained in service until retired by VO-4 in May 1946. NAS Norfolk crew prepares to arm OS2U-3 with depth charges c. 1942. *US Navy*

Yorktown (CV-10) steams at high speed through the Caribbean Sea off Trinidad during her spring 1943 shakedown cruise with Air Group Five embarked. *US Navy/LT Charles Kerlee, courtesy Russ Egnor*

We found a large concentration south of Arles and the entire flight made numerous rocket and strafing runs from a low altitude. Many fires and secondary explosions were seen but we pressed on with the attack. During one of the strafing runs I felt a hit and saw a hole in my right wing. Bub called and said he had been hit, so we pulled out of the immediate combat area to inspect each other's damage. I was OK but when I saw many holes behind the cockpit in Bub's plane, I told him that they almost missed him. He said, "Yeah?" and waved to me through the top of his canopy, which had been shot away.

At that moment I heard and saw exploding flak above my head and another off my wingtip. We made a violent turn to evade the flak, which was at about 1,000 feet. During the turn we were looking straight down, and below us at treetop level were three Ju-52s heading south. I was in position for a classic high side run, so I closed and began firing at the plane on the right.

Damn! I was out of ammunition in four guns, and the right wing gun I had been saving had been hit during the strafing runs. That gun was firing but it looked as if the tracers were tumbling end over end, yet the plane on the right peeled off and went down. The other two Ju-52s had split up with Bub chasing the second. Luckily, I could still see the third so I closed and made high side runs, firing at the right engine. With only one gun firing properly, nothing was happening and I felt frustrated until I saw the right propeller fly off. The plane went into a violent skid, hitting the ground in an open field. I saw a man in a white shirt, presumably the pilot, get out and run into a ditch. I strafed the plane with no further results.

By this time I was somewhat lost and I was separated from Bub and the rest of the flight. I saw fire about five miles away, which was the plane Bub had shot down, so I climbed hoping to rejoin with Bub. But at 1,000 feet the sky turned black with flak and I headed for the treetops, and as I leveled out I felt another thump. Some of my instruments were on zero and there was another hole in my wing. I called Bub and told him I might have a bad hit and I was heading for home.

Although somewhat lost, I knew the Mediterranean was south, and if I was going down I wanted to be over water, not land. Each time I climbed for more altitude I drew flak so I stayed at treetop level until I reached the sea. By that time oil was coming into the cockpit deck and I was more concerned. I climbed to 1,000 feet and began to take my bearings when I saw a Spitfire

69

Three Douglas R4D Skytrain transports of VR-7 in formation off the coast of Florida shortly after the squadron's 4 Apr 1943 establishment as NAS Jacksonville. *US Navy, courtesy Don S. Montgomery*

Free French officer at Port Lyautey, and K-109 was lost at its mooring in violent winds. But replacements were dispatched and safely arrived, bringing to eight the number of K-ships which crossed the Atlantic. They remain the only nonrigid aircraft to perform that feat, giving ZP-14 a monopoly on the world record which lasted until blimps were retired from the Navy in 1961.

One other aspect of naval aviation in the European war merits mention. By Act of Congress, the Coast Guard functions as part of the Navy in time of war. President Roosevelt jumped the gun a bit when he ordered the Coast Guard placed under Navy operational control on 1 November 1941, but it mattered little. By then his administration was supporting covert operations against both Germany and Japan.

Some Navy officers expressed mild surprise at how efficiently the "Coasties" made the transition from peace to war. By definition and tradition, the service is dedicated to saving lives, and some military professionals have noted an ingrained streak of pacifism in the "revenue service." But that very portion of the job had frequently brought Coast Guardsmen into violent con-

flict with seagoing outlaws—mainly liquor smugglers during the prohibition period of the 1920s.

Coast Guard aviation has always been extremely small; in 1941, it was absolutely minuscule. The service's aviation branch during World War II involved nine air stations and one operational squadron, though each air base had planes assigned for patrol and liaison purposes.

The only USCG unit actively engaged in offensive operations was Patrol Bombing Squadron Six, flying PBY-5s from Greenland and Iceland. But in concert with aircraft assigned to stateside air stations, it made its presence felt. From 1942 on, Coast Guard aviators conducted 61 attacks on hostile or unidentified submarines. But more in keeping with the service's primary mission, its aircraft located 1,000 or more survivors of torpedoed ships and actually rescued almost 100.

The most common operational aircraft were Vought OS2U Kingfisher floatplanes and Grumman J2F Duck amphibians. However, an exceptional event occurred on 1 August 1942 when an armed Grumman J4F Widgeon from

USCG pilot Chief Aviation Pilot Henry C. White and Radioman First Class George H. Boggs, Jr., scored Coast Guard aviation's only submarine kill of WWII while flying this Grumman J4F-1 Widgeon, SerNo V215, over the Gulf of Mexico about 100 miles off Houma, La., 1 Aug 1942. *Rudy Arnold, courtesy Stan Piet*

Houma, Louisiana, sank U-166 off the mouth of the Mississippi River.

Undoubtedly the most innovative aspect of USCG aviation involved helicopters. Interest in helos dated from April 1942 with a demonstration of Igor Sikorsky's XR-4. Three Sikorsky HNS-1s (identical to the Army's R-4) were delivered to NAS Floyd Bennett Field in New York, and in December 1943 the local Coast Guard detachment prepared to conduct formal classes the following month. By that fall the station had thirteen helos, including some British aircraft and students.

Almost forgotten is the fact that Coast Guard aviators performed one of the world's first helicopter rescues. A Canadian transport plane had crashed 125 miles from Goose Bay, Labrador, in April 1945, stranding most of its crew. The melting spring snow prevented further rescue attempts by ski-equipped aircraft, and eleven men remained marooned in the rugged, inaccessible terrain. To complicate matters, one rescue plane had been wrecked, leaving two more men at the scene.

One of the Floyd Bennett Sikorskis was dismantled, stowed in an Army C-54 transport and ferried 1,000 miles to Labrador. There the HNS-1 was reassembled and began a series of staging flights into the crash site, where the men had waited for two weeks. It was slow going—the HNS cruised at 57 mph and had only one passenger seat—but the job was completed within five days of notification. Six Coast Guardsmen received decorations for this feat, including the helo pilot, Lieutenant August Kleisch.

Helicopters did not regularly operate from ships until shortly after World War II, but the first deployment of an aircraft carrier with an assigned helo was made with a Coast Guard aircraft and pilot.

Coast Guard Sikorsky HSN-1 Hoverfly during a rescue demonstration at CGAS Floyd Bennett Field c. 1943. The Coast Guard pioneered development of helicopters for naval service following the Navy's acquisition of a USAAF YR-4B (USN HNS-1) in July 1942. In April 1945, a Coast Guard helicopter performed one of the world's first helo rescues. *US Navy, courtesy Doug Siegfried*

Marine Scouting Squadron Three Douglas SBD-5 Dauntlesses flying from MCAS Bourne Field, St. Thomas, Virgin Islands, during May 1944. The squadron was one of 15 inshore patrol squadrons assigned to defend East Coast and Caribbean shipping from U-boat attacks. *US Navy*

Though naval aviation played a significant role in the Battle of the Atlantic, no Marine Corps squadrons flew against Germany—contrary to policy in the First War. An SBD squadron, VMS-3, flew ASW patrols out of the Virgin Islands until May 1944 but saw very little activity. It was no accident.

The reasons were twofold: the Corps' primary responsibility in the Pacific and a grim determination by the Army to keep flying leathernecks out of the European Theater of Operations (ETO). Lingering resentment of "devil dog" headlines in World War I (at the expense of General Pershing's doughboys) was remembered by a generation of Army officers.

However, during the summer of 1944, a full Marine aircraft group, MAG-51, was alerted for training in a special ETO mission. The 8th Army Air Force was involved in Operation Crossbow—a concerted effort to destroy V-1 flying bomb sites in France—but enjoyed minimal success. Consequently, MAG-51 undertook the Marine Corps part of the program, known as Project Danny.

The Death of "Danny"

Commander Thomas Moorer—a former F3F and PBY pilot—was involved in Project Danny, a plan to attack German robot-bomb sites in France. The reaction he received during a joint service briefing is as surprising now as it must have been then.

I was on the NavAirLant staff, and the mission Washington wanted done was to destroy the V-1 launchers which were wreaking havoc in London. Working with the Marine air staff at Cherry Point, N.C., we developed a plan to use six Marine F4U squadrons, each airplane armed with Tiny Tim rockets. At that time, these airborne rockets were the largest anywhere in the world, and carried a heavy punch in a 11.75 inch projectile. Our plan was to put the six Marine squadrons on jeep carriers, sail to Europe, and launch the F4Us from the North Sea to make a series of massive attacks on the Nazi targets.

After all the planning was done, the training was in progress, and the logistics were in order, I was sent to Washington with a group to brief the highest civilian and military authorities, including General George C. Marshall (the Army chief of staff). It was my first trip to the newly built Pentagon. The conference room was filled with brass, and only General Marshall was momentarily absent. I was told to go ahead with my briefing. I got well into it, when General Marshall entered the room. I stopped and everybody rose in deference to America's most prestigious military figure.

One of his staff generals quickly summarized my briefing to that point. General Marshall listened, but on hearing that US Marine aviators would make the planned attacks, he raised his hand.

The Aviation ordnancemen of WWII were responsible for arming aircraft and maintenance of weapons. The "redshirts," as they were also known because of their red jerseys worn during flight quarters, were vital to the success of the missions of carrier aircraft. Ordnancemen load bombs into Grumman TBF-1 Avengers c. mid-1942. *US Navy, courtesy Russ Egnor*

Rising to his feet, he moved toward the door and said something to the effect, "That's the end of this briefing. As long as I'm in charge of our armed forces, there will never be a Marine in Europe."

And there never was during World War II.

After the war, Moorer coauthored the Pacific portion of the Strategic Bombing Survey. Later he rose to Chief of Naval Operations during the Vietnam War and became Chairman of the Joint Chiefs under President Nixon.

Despite such interservice rivalry, the Battle of the Atlantic was won. For naval aviation, however, the major effort was focused on the other side of the globe, where the Navy's major war had begun: in the Pacific.

Also serving in the Aleutians were Consolidated's PBY Catalinas. However, the "Cat" earned its real fame in the South Pacific with the "Black Cat" squadrons and their nocturnal missions in the Solomons. PBY-5A is on a 1942–43 patrol mission from Attu. *US Navy*

utility unit. Three seaplane tenders serviced the PatRons while the utility squadron performed ordinary chores with assorted floatplanes.

The men of PatWing Ten held no illusions about their prospects of surviving a Japanese fighter attack in a slow-climbing Catalina. They sang, "You can't get to heaven in a PBY, 'cause a PBY don't fly that high."

Asiatic Fleet headquarters in Manila learned of the Pearl Harbor attack at 0300 on 8 December, local time. Four hours later, the tender *William B. Preston* (AVD-7) in Davao Gulf reported that she was under air attack. Two PBYs were sunk, and the war was on. Half a century later,

Right
Douglas SBD-1 Dauntlesses of VMSB-132 in flight near Quantico, Va., soon after the squadron's 1 July 1941 redesignation from VMB-1. The Marine bombing squadron entered combat at Guadalcanal in October 1942.

historians search in vain for an explanation as to why American forces in the Philippines were surprised several hours after events in Hawaii.

However, the squadrons coped as best they could. Aircraft were dispersed to lakes, coves, and swamps, as PBYs and floatplanes could still operate when airfields were bombed or strafed with near impunity.

Boeing's bid to produce a long-range patrol bomber flying boat for the Navy resulted in only one aircraft, the XPBB-1 Ranger which first flew 9 Jul 1942. Although the aircraft had excellent performance characteristics, the Navy's future requirements for seaplane patrol bombers were changed and the PBB was cancelled, leaving the prototype to be dubbed "The Lone Ranger." *Boeing*

A handful of offensive missions were undertaken with bombs or torpedoes, but the PBYs continued suffering losses without compensating damage to the enemy. Attrition was unrelenting, seven Catalinas on 12 December alone. Sixteen surviving aircraft withdrew to the Dutch East Indies, operating from two tenders briefly before Japanese naval-air forces overwhelmed the Anglo-Dutch-American defenders. The last straw was drawn on 27 February when *Langley* (AV-3), converted from America's first aircraft carrier into a seaplane tender, was sunk ferrying Army fighters to Java.

A handful of PatWing Ten planes finally fetched up in Australia, leaving behind 35 destroyed in action, crashed, or damaged beyond repair. Twenty-four pilots, including seven noncommissioned aviators, had been killed or were missing.

In exchange, the PBYs had sunk a Japanese freighter and damaged a transport and two warships.

Patrol Wing Ten had been doomed from the start; outnumbered, lacking fighter escort, with no hope of resupply. The Catalina crews and their support personnel were chronically short of everything—everything, that is, except the willingness to hang on.

That same gritty determination was evident at tiny Wake Island, 1,000 miles from Japan. Marine Fighting Squadron 211 lost all but five of its F4F-3s the first day of the war, and soon was reduced to four flyable Wildcats. Aside from half the squadron killed or wounded, most of the supplies, ammunition, and fuel was destroyed in the first attack.

But for more than two weeks Major Paul Putnam's officers and men worked minor miracles of improvisation, keeping a handful of fighters available to intercept almost daily bombing raids. VMF-211 shot down at least six enemy aircraft and, with gunners of the defense battalion, sank two Japanese ships and repulsed the first enemy landing attempt. In the second, 23 December, Captain Henry Elrod died fighting on foot. Retroactively he became the first naval aviator awarded the Medal of Honor in World War II.

The men of PatWing Ten and Fighting 211 demonstrated genuine heroism—a concept severely diluted and trivialized in the half century since the fall of the Philippines and Wake Island. Unless the risk of failure in an endeavor involves death, dismemberment, or torture, it should be called something else because it is not heroic. But heroism alone would not reverse the appalling losses suffered at Japanese hands in the early months of the Pacific war. The first step was for the American nation to acknowledge reality. The Japanese armed forces were not invincible, but they required unstinting respect. It took a while for many Americans to grasp that fact.

Japan, though a small, isolated island nation, possessed two important advantages. Strategically, she benefited from uni-

Assigned to Fleet Air Wing One as part of the inshore patrol squadron force, these VS-51 Douglas SBD-5 Dauntlesses are on a flight out of Tutuila, Samoa, during May 1944. *US Navy*

Bombing 11 Douglas SBD-3 Dauntless is positioned on board a Pacific Fleet carrier during workups in late 1942. A unit of CVG-11, which was scheduled for assignment to *Hornet* (CV-8), VB-11 was instead shifted to Guadalcanal after *Hornet* was sunk 26 October 1942. Returning to the United States in July 1943, the squadron began its first carrier deployment in the new *Hornet* (CV-12) during October 1944, flying Curtiss SB2C Helldivers. *US Navy*

fied command and the option to strike wherever she chose. The Allied forces were widely dispersed, lacking central command and control, with virtually no experience in operating together. The Battle of the Java Sea in February 1942 proved as much: the impromptu American-British-Dutch-Australian naval force was soundly defeated by the unified Japanese.

Additionally, Japan had an important tactical advantage. The Imperial Navy boasted nine aircraft carriers in the fall of 1941. The US Pacific Fleet had only three, and the British dispatched just one to the Indian Ocean. The latter, HMS *Hermes*, was sunk by Japanese aircraft off Ceylon in April.

Almost immediately after Pearl Harbor, a fourth carrier joined the Pacific Fleet. She was *Yorktown*, elder sister of *Enterprise*. Transferred from the Atlantic, "Yorky" proved invaluable for the first six months of the new year. And then she died.

Despite technical and numerical deficiencies, the PacFleet carriers possessed an invaluable asset: high-quality leadership. It began at the squadron level, exemplified by junior and middle-grade officers such as Lieutenant Commanders Paul Ramsey (VF-2) and John Waldron (VT-8) and Lieutenant Richard H. Best (VB-6). Perhaps best-known to the public was Lieutenant Commander John S. Thach of Fighting Three. Hailing from Fordyce, Arkansas, "Jimmy" Thach was a 37-year-old lieutenant commander in 1942 with extensive aviation experience. Thach

had maneuvered matchsticks around his kitchen table in Coronado, California, devising the defensive fighter tactics credited with saving untold naval aviators throughout the war.

Like many gifted leaders, Thach was also a talented teacher. No one absorbed the skipper's lessons better than Lieutenant (jg) Edward H. O'Hare, who would become an ace and earn the Medal of Honor in a furious few minutes defending *Lexington* from land-based bombers on 20 February. O'Hare, in turn, became an exceptional leader and mentor himself.

Below
LTJG Edw. H. "Butch" O'Hare, became the first naval aviator to be awarded a Medal of Honor in WWII. As a member of VF-3, O'Hare was credited with virtually single-handedly saving *Lexington* (CV-2) from an attack 20 February 1942 by eight twin-engine Mitsubishi G4M1 Type I (later "Betty") bombers. O'Hare was officially credited with five kills and one probable during the flight. He later, as Commander Air Group Six, was killed in a night engagement. *US Navy*

Freshly camouflaged, *Hornet* (CV-8) stands out of Pearl Harbor during summer 1942. On 28 Aug she made her last sortie from Pearl to participate in the battle for Guadalcanal. A veteran of Midway, *Hornet* was lost during the Battle of Santa Cruz 26 Oct 1942. *US Navy, courtesy Don S. Montgomery*

With few exceptions, air group and staff leadership was equally as good as the squadron level. But task force command would prove erratic. Only 20 years separated the combat challenge of 1942 from *Langley's* fragile origins; those two decades were insufficient for early aviators to grow stars on their collars. Consequently, some senior captains (Ernest King and William Halsey, among them) had gone through basic flight training in the 1930s (Halsey insisted on a complete course). The "black-shoe" (surface officer) and "brownshoe" (aviator) feud should have been resolved on or about 7 December, but the "gun club" members of the battleship Navy conceded little.

Combat experience would demonstrate that even the best commanders required experience and seasoning. Nonaviator Frank Jack Fletcher commanded carriers in the first three flattop battles, proving competent but frequently indecisive. At Midway, he turned over tactical control to Rear Raymond A. Spruance, a cruiser officer who had inherited his staff from ailing "Bull" Halsey. And Ray Spruance conducted a masterpiece of a battle.

That fall, Rear Admiral Thomas C. Kinkaid was officer in tactical command off the Solomons. Like Fletcher, he was not an aviator and had far less practical experience than "Fletch." Kinkaid's handling of the Santa Cruz battle has been widely criticized, but he bounced back to prominence as an amphibious commander.

The Imperial Japanese Navy faced a similar leadership dilemma. The fleet commander, Admiral Isoroku Yamamoto, was an early naval aviation advocate, but few of his task group or even carrier commanders wore wings. Again, tactical units and staff aviators made up the deficit. Naval air battles were decided as they had been since the days of oars and sail: on the basis of weapons and tactics, leadership and courage, and the priceless asset called luck.

Ironically, US carrier aviation's first significant blow in World War II required Army aircraft. In a stunning example of joint-service innovation, sixteen twin-engine B-25 bombers attacked Japanese cities with minimal ordnance. The goal was never to inflict strategic damage—that was clearly impossible so early in the war. But the First Special Aviation Project would boost American morale and demonstrate Japanese vulnerability.

The mission was conceived, organized, and led by Lieutenant Colonel James H. Doolittle, a supremely versatile pilot, engineer, and leader. After specialized training in carrier launch procedures, the Army aircrews boarded *Hornet* (CV-8) in California and sailed for the Western Pacific.

Detected by Japanese picket boats, the Mitchell bombers launched prematurely on 18 April. They inflicted widespread but minimal damage on military and industrial targets in Tokyo, Yokohama, and Nagoya, then headed for the China coast. Fifteen B-25s were lost to weather or fuel exhaustion before reaching their briefed landing sites; the other was interned in Russia.

Stung by the Doolittle raid, Tokyo's general staff resolved to draw the remaining US carriers into decisive combat. Thus was set the stage for the climactic Battle of Midway. But preliminary steps were already in motion.

In the spring of 1942, the principles of carrier warfare were understood by both navies. As in most forms of warfare, the first rule was to strike first. Reversing the biblical phrase, Americans said, "Do unto others before they do unto you." This dictum assumed even greater importance in carrier warfare because of the physical nature of the ship. Concentrated in one small area were extremely volatile materials: gasoline, ordnance, and fuel oil. Ignition of any item could spark a chain reaction which would doom the ship. Additionally, the carrier's narrow flight deck could be rendered inoperable by two or three bombs. Torpedo damage was more likely to put a CV out of action if a list developed which went uncorrected. While both bomb and torpedo damage could sometimes be quickly repaired, in most forms of aerial warfare, time is the commodity in shortest supply.

Therefore, scouting and communications loomed large in the carrier equation. Tactically, reconnaissance was probably the greatest difference between US and Japanese carrier doctrine. The Imperial Navy emphasized maximum strike capability in its air

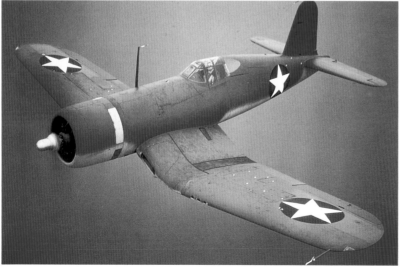

Above
The big Grumman Hellcat just arrived on the West Coast with VF-3 at NAS San Diego, Calif., in April 1943 and then VF-4 at NAS Alameda, Calif., in June. These two early-production -3s over San Francisco Bay in 1943 indicate they were probably assigned to VF-4. *US Navy, courtesy Russ Egnor*

Left
Although the first flight of Vought's XF4U-1 Corsair was made 29 May 1940, it didn't make it to the fleet until reporting to VF-12 on 3 October 1942 at NAS San Diego, California. Initial carrier trial difficulties led to a lack of faith in the powerful fighter as a carrier aircraft and it won its first combat fame with land-based USN/USMC units in the Solomons. *US Navy, courtesy Jeff Ethell*

Fighting 12 was the first Navy squadron to receive the Vought F4U-1 Corsair, which they flew land-based stateside in a training status Moving to the Solomons in June 1943 and acquiring F6F-3s VF-12 took the Hellcat into combat in November from *Saratoga* (CV-3) at Bouganville. Completing its first combat tour in June 1944, VF-12 re-formed and returned to the Pacific in *Randolph* (CV-15) during January 1945 with new F6F-5s, as seen here. *US Navy, courtesy Don S. Montgomery*

groups, leaving most scouting missions to battleship and cruiser-based floatplanes. Thus, dive bombers and torpedo planes were freed for attack missions. However, American air groups devoted one-quarter of their strength to a dedicated scout-bomber squadron.

Whatever deficiencies existed in American equipment—particularly aerial torpedoes and VT aircraft—the US Navy possessed one big advantage. The Anglo-American scientific alliance had produced seagoing radar, which proved invaluable in detecting hostile aircraft. Japan seldom had such equipment in the first year of the war. Combined with improvements in voice radio, ship-based radar enabled the new science of carrier fighter direction.

Strike doctrine in both navies adhered to the Clausewitzian principle of mass. Ideally, once an enemy force was located, at least one full air group would launch a coordinated strike with dive bombers and torpedo planes. The object was to split the antiaircraft guns and defending fighters, while the attack group's escorts engaged enemy interceptors. It was a fine theory, and it worked when implemented in sufficient strength.

But in practice, the theory was seldom realized during 1942. On 7 May, first day of the Coral Sea battle, 93 planes from *Lexington* and *Yorktown* attacked the Japanese light carrier *Shoho*. The two air groups overwhelmed the defense and quickly sank

Grumman J2F-5 Duck and Douglas SBD-3P Dauntless of VJ-14 at NAS Moffet Field, California, in 1943. Grumman's Duck entered service as the JF-1 during 1934 and served until after WWII when finally retired from the Reserves and Coast Guard in 1948. *Bill Reed, courtesy Tom Doll*

the small carrier, even though she was protected by four cruisers and a destroyer. It remained the only fully coordinated US air strike during the four carrier battles of 1942.

The Japanese, however, mounted some well-organized attacks, but of smaller composition. The following day *Lexington* was lost and *Yorktown* damaged in a determined Japanese strike from the large carriers *Shokaku* and *Zuikaku*, both of which had attacked Pearl Harbor. Simultaneous US attacks hunted through worsening weather, which dispersed squadrons of SBD scout-bombers and TBD torpedo planes. Some Dauntlesses and Devastators found their targets but scored with no torpedoes and few bombs.

Though Japan could claim a tactical victory, the strategic implications of Coral Sea favored the Allies. Japan's drive against Port Moresby, New Guinea, was blunted, thus denying the enemy a springboard toward northern Australia.

Coral Sea was historically significant as well. For the first time in millennia of naval warfare, a sea battle had been fought without opposing ships sighting one another. Conducted wholly "below the horizon" by carrier aircraft, the two-day engagement set the pace for future combat in the Pacific.

Naval aviation's second and third Medals of Honor were earned at Coral Sea. Two SBD pilots received the nation's highest decoration for their actions on 8 May: Lieutenant Joseph J. Powers of *Yorktown's* VB-5 and Lieutenant (jg) William E. Hall of *Lexington's* VS-2. "Jojo" Powers' medal was awarded posthumously following his determined attack against *Shokaku;* while Hall, though wounded, continued defending "Lex" from enemy aircraft.

Of the four carrier battles in 1942, only Midway proved a clear-cut tactical and strategic victory for either side. Fought one month after Coral Sea, the engagement pitted *Enterprise, Hornet,*

"The Iron Works," Grumman Aircraft Engineering Corp., was most noted for its WWII fighters, but it also produced some of the Navy's most successful utility planes, such as this JRF-5 Goose on a factory flight in 1943. *Rudy Arnold, courtesy Stan Piet*

VJ-14 operated several versions of the Martin Marauder for utility roles from NAS Moffett Field, California, including JM-1Ps modified for photographic missions. VJ-14 JM-1s on Moffett ramp in 1943. *Bill Reed, courtesy Tom Doll*

and hastily repaired *Yorktown* against four of Vice Admiral Chuichi Nagumo's veterans, plus dozens of surface combatants.

As much as anything, Midway was a victory of American intelligence. Navy code breakers discerned enough of enemy intentions to give Pacific Fleet commander Chester Nimitz the crucial edge he needed to deny Japan a foothold in the Hawaiian Islands. Ironically, this most significant of all carrier battles was orchestrated by Nimitz, a submariner, while his task force commanders—Frank Jack Fletcher and Raymond A. Spruance—were both blackshoe surface officers.

However, the PacFleet and task force commanders had excellent subordinates. Fletcher had ridden *Yorktown* since

Below
Between 1939 and 1942 the Navy's aircraft went through a variety of paint schemes and national insignia design in order to find the best protection for aircrews. These Vought OS2U-3 Kingfishers wear the scheme and markings of early 1942. *NASM*

The Panama Canal was America's vital link between the Atlantic and Pacific Oceans, enabling the Navy's new Fast Carriers to quickly transfer to the Pacific Theater after completing their shakedown cruises on the East Coast. *Yorktown* (CV-10) transits "The Ditch" 11 July 1943 with CVG-5 embarked. *US Navy, courtesy Stan Piet*

shortly after Pearl Harbor while Spruance inherited Bull Halsey's experienced if mercurial staff. *Enterprise* and *Yorktown* flew competent, battle-tested air groups, though *Hornet* took a back seat. Only her torpedo squadron found significant combat, losing all 15 TBDs and five of six land-based TBFs on the morning of 4 June.

The other two TorpRons also suffered appalling losses. Between them, VT-3 and -6 lost 22 additional Devastators, com-

pounding the damage inflicted on Marine Corps land-based aircraft and upon Midway itself.

"Slow Down and Let Them Shoot at You"

Wilhelm G. Esders was an enlisted pilot who joined Torpedo Squadron Three in 1938. Though originally a *Saratoga* squadron, VT-3 was temporarily assigned to *Yorktown* for the Battle of Midway, led by Lieutenant Commander Lance E. Massey.

Consolidated PB2Y Coronados under final phase of construction at the company's San Diego, California, plant in July 1943. Still wary of aerial attacks from the Japanese, the work area is covered by camouflage netting. The giant Coronado was produced as a patrol bomber, but some were modified to transports and evacuation aircraft. *US Navy/Jacobs, courtesy Russ Egnor*

Wasp Air Group is readied for launch from CV-7 during August 1942. Grumman F4F-4 Wildcats of VF-71 and Douglas SBD-3 Dauntlessess of VS-71/72 are shown. VT-71's Grumman TBF-1 Avengers are absent. *Wasp* was sunk 15 September 1942 after she was mortally wounded by a Japanese submarine during the battle for Guadalcanal. Abandoned, but stubbornly refusing to sink, *Wasp* was finally destroyed by torpedoes from a US destroyer. *LTJG John R. Prann, USN, courtesy T.J. Wilkes*

On the morning of 4 June, pilots of VT-3 were in their ready room before daylight, awaiting a good fix on the Japanese fleet. We were briefed on the weather and were told we would make a standard torpedo attack that we had practiced for years. We had very highly trained pilots, and may have been the most highly trained in the fleet. We were ready to give all, as it was stated to the air group that the future of the United States depended on the approximately 250 pilots in the three carriers.

After launch and rendezvous, we headed for the enemy fleet in company of other Yorktown squadrons. The enemy force was eventually sighted and VT-3 altered course slightly to the right. When we were still more than 12 miles from the enemy fleet we were attacked by Zeros. Descending, jinking as much as possible in formation, while all the time increasing speed, didn't help our situation. I could hear bullets going through the fuselage and a 20mm explosive round hit the armor plate on the back of my seat. Another 20mm hit elsewhere in the plane, but I didn't know until my radioman-gunner, ARM2/c Mike Brazier, called that he wouldn't be able to help defend us; he had been badly wounded.

About this time I observed three Zeros lined up on the starboard bow. They were in position to hit both the skipper and myself in one pass. I immediately pulled up about 10 feet. I saw tracers going into Lieutenant Commander Massey's plane but passing under mine. All at once the skipper's plane was a big ball of fire; he immediately stood up, one foot on the stub wing and the other on the seat. At this time he passed out of sight under my wing;

we were at about 250 feet. I feel he was going to use his parachute, but at that altitude it was improbable that it would be effective.

Now, there I was out in front of the squadron, but what should I do—fall in line behind the second division and let the XO lead the attack, or take over the lead? Having made many practice

"Blueshirts" position a Douglas SBD Dauntless on the hangar deck of an escort carrier. Navy flight deck and hangar deck personnel are identified by the color of their jerseys worn at flight quarters. Blueshirts are plane handlers, while brownshirts (in cockpit) are plane captains. *US Navy*

dropping down from above, came the air group commander and VS-6, usurping our target. The three-plane CAG section, followed by Scouting Six, came over the top and down, barely missing our first section. Only a blur was visible as the diving SBDs blanked out our forward view. This caused Best to scramble out of the way before we became victims of a large midair collision.

Baker Two and Three followed B-1 while B-5 and -6 went their own way. It was a good thing one cool head prevailed in this fiasco, for the skipper radioed VB-6 to follow him to the next

Below
Flight decks are one of the most dangerous working environments in the world. Closely supervising the flight decks are the "yellowshirts," which include the Aircraft Handler (officer in charge of the flight deck), senior officer and enlisted personnel, as well as aircraft directors. On board a training CVE off San Diego, California, c. 1943, the flight deck bos'n briefs a group of "greenshirts," which include catapult and arresting gear personnel, along with photographers and aircraft technicians. *US Navy*

The "Hot Poppas," wearing heavy asbestos protective suits, risked their lives to rescue pilots and aircrewmen from burning aircraft during emergency situations. *US Navy*

carrier in line. His decision could have been one of the crucial acts of the battle. Though only the first section of VB-6 attacked the second carrier—probably IJNS Akagi—those three planes destroyed the ship and its air group. Otherwise, the Japanese would have continued the battle with two carriers instead of just one.

The remaining VB-6 pilots either did not hear the CO's radio command or they were confused and followed Scouting Six in attacking the nearer ship, evidently Kaga.

Leaving the area of the snafu, I resumed facing aft with my twin .30s ready, even though no enemy fighters were seen. The only planes following us were B-2 and -3. We approached the

second carrier from the southwest, about 45 degrees relative to the ship's heading. I felt the plane slowing, indicating that the dive flaps had been opened and that we were approaching the roll-in point. Lieutenant (jg) Kroeger and Ensign Weber had taken the proper interval, still without a Zero in sight. I could see smoke rising from Kaga and, in the distance, another carrier under attack from a dive-bombing squadron. (This was VB-3, which apparently struck Soryu.) I stowed the .30s and again faced forward.

Baker One was at 15,000 feet when we rolled into our dive, followed by B-2 and -3. Looking through the pilot's windscreen, I could see the big red "meatball" on a somewhat dirty *yellow deck. A fighter was just launching with another in line, while farther aft more aircraft awaited launch. My thoughts went back to 7 December, and I pondered that the Japanese pilots never thought this could ever happen to them or their ships.*

I began reading off the altitude over the intercom around 6,000 feet, in 1,000-foot increments. This would allow the skipper to concentrate on the target without watching his own

At the time of the attack on Pearl Harbor, the US Navy had no blimps on the West Coast. The first airships reported to the Pacific Fleet in 1942 at NAS Moffett Field, California—these were four former Goodyear advertising blimps dubbed L-ships. The first West Coast LTA squadron was ZP-32, established 31 January 1942 at Moffett. This Goodyear K-ship is moored at NAS Quillayute, Washington, c. 1944-1945.

WWII maintenance and ordnance personnel on carriers came from various sources such as carrier maintenance shops, CASUs (Carrier Aircraft Service Units), or from the individual squadrons. Aviation Ordnancemen, such as these seen working on a TBM turret gun, would normally wear red jerseys during flight quarters. *US Navy, courtesy Jeff Ethell*

altimeter. Our plane must have been spotted, because 40- and 20mm tracers started coming up from the carrier. The shells rising toward B-1 were passing over and beyond the port wing. At 2,000 feet, the normal release point, I changed to 100-foot increments. I felt the bomb leave the plane just before I called 1,500. Then, as we pulled out, I was pushed down in my seat.

We passed over Akagi between the island and the starboard bow. I could see the crew scurrying about the bridge and on the deck. Now, looking aft again with my guns ready, I expected the Zero CAP to come after us. But they didn't appear. Lieutenant Best banked so we could see where our bomb struck, and we both swore that it landed midships in the forward group of planes, abreast of the island. Another bomb exploded in the planes near the fantail. Immediately thereafter, flaming planes were hurled every which way and a huge fire broke out.

Kroeger's bomb apparently landed on the port bow deck edge and splashed water over the ship. Weber's bomb hit among the planes on the flight deck aft.

As Kroeger took position on our wing he was really beaming and gave me the OK sign. Weber in B-3 joined momentarily so

USMC North American PBJ-1H Mitchell during a company test flight c. 1944. Deliveries of Marine versions of the USAAF B-25 began in 1943. Variations between Army Air Force and Marine Corps versions varied little and the Army suffix letter corresponded to the Marine version-the PBJ-1H was equivalent to the USAAF B-25H. In November 1944, a PBJ-1H was launched and recovered during carrier suitability trials from *Shangri-la* (CV-38). *North American, courtesy Gene Boswell*

the first section of Bombing Six was intact. No other VB-6 planes were visible, in fact they had not been seen since they deployed for the attack. But what a bombing feat! Three planes, three claimed hits, and the huge carrier Akagi, *flagship of the Japanese Carrier Striking Force, spectacularly on fire. Its air group was destroyed on deck.*

Still on the lookout for enemy fighters, I could see three Japanese carriers dead in the water, belching smoke and flames. If only I'd had a camera—it would surely have been one of the greatest photos of the Pacific war.

Jim Murray was commissioned in 1943 and served the rest of the war in aviation maintenance positions. He retired as a commander in 1957 and eventually settled in San Diego, where he passed away in 1989.

Though *Yorktown* was lost to a combination of air and submarine attacks, Midway survived. Imperial Japan had lost not only her first naval battle in 350 years, she lost her strategic momentum, never to regain it.

Only 60 days after Midway, on 7 August, American naval forces began their first offensive of the war. The object was an obscure island in the Solomons group, south of the equator. Its name was Guadalcanal.

Navy and Marine Corps aviation were intimately involved in the Guadalcanal campaign, which officially ran until February 1943. Carriers were crucial, and two flattop duels were fought in those six months of nonstop combat.

A naval-air engagement developed on 24 August, barely two weeks after the landings at Guadalcanal and Tulagi. The Japanese lost the light carrier *Ryujo* in the Battle of the Eastern Solomons when *Saratoga* SBDs and TBFs overwhelmed the enemy force. In response, Coral Sea veterans *Shokaku* and *Zuikaku* hit Task Force 61, damaging "The Big E." However, American tailhook aviators had preserved the status quo ashore—as good as a victory for the increasingly beleaguered leathernecks.

Meanwhile, Marine fighter and scout-bomber squadrons trickled into Guadalcanal's Henderson Field, named for a squadron commander killed at Midway. Finding almost daily combat, the hard-pressed Wildcat pilots struggled up to altitude with every report from the coastwatcher network farther up the Solomons. These battles produced the first major American fighter aces of the war: Major John L. Smith and Captain Marion E. Carl of VMF-223. They were ably supported by Major Robert E. Galer's VMF-224 and replacements from Lieutenant Colonel Harold Bauer's -212.

Nor were Navy FitRons neglected. During the campaign, *Saratoga's* displaced Fighting Five under Lieutenant Commander Leroy Simpler fought alongside the Marines, as did *Enterprise's* VF-10 of Lieutenant Commander James H. Flatley. In October VMF-121 arrived in strength, and its executive officer skyrocketed to fame. Major Joseph J. Foss became not only the naval service's leading fighter pilot, but the first World War II ace to match Captain Eddie Rickenbacker's Great War record of 26 victories.

Navy and Marine SBDs comprised the primary striking arm of the "Cactus Air Force," beginning with Lieutenant Colonel Richard C. Mangrum's VMSB-232. Sinking or deterring Japanese seaborne reinforcement was the primary mission of the Dauntless squadrons, but most of them paid a high price. Major Gordon Bell's VMSB-141 lost all its senior aviators in one hellish night of naval bombardment, and there were mornings when only one SBD remained operational on the island.

Surviving "Cactus"

Major Richard C. Mangrum was a veteran Marine aviator at the time of Pearl Harbor. With tours in fighters, scout-bombers, and flight training, he logged some 3,000 hours before assuming command of VMSB-232 in preparation for joining Guadalcanal's "Cactus Air Force."

I moved up to command the squadron in January 1942. For the next six months we trained with what we could get, mostly SBD-2s handed down from the carriers as they acquired new-production SBD-3s. New pilots trickled in slowly, as did new enlisted personnel, and squadrons subdivided like amoeba forming new units. With five officers of varying experience, I acquired around 1 July ten new second lieutenants fresh from accelerated flight training, and their average flight time was some 250 hours—none in SBDs.

On 5 July VMSB-232 was alerted for the South Pacific and obtained 12 new SBD-3s from the fleet pool; there weren't any more. Normal complement at that time would have been 18. Normal pilot complement for 18 airplanes later became 53—I went to Guadalcanal with 15!

The next 30 days was a period of frantic shakedown of pilots and planes, and rear-seat gunners. We also included carrier qualification for the new pilots. Tools and spare parts were practically nonexistent, and we had to make do with what little

Newly commissioned VMSB-241 (1 Mar 42) flew mix of Vought SB2U-3 Vindicators, recently acquired from VMSB-231, and Douglas SBD-2 Dauntlesses; at the Battle of Midway. Still photo taken from a motion picture filmed at Midway shows two-241 Vindicators on takeoff for a training mission shortly before the 4 June 1942 battle. VMSB-241 sustained heavy losses and one SB2U pilot, CAPT Richard E. Fleming, was posthumously awarded the Medal of Honor from his actions. *US Navy*

Fleet Air Wing One Martin PBM-3 Mariner is refueled at Saipan c. 1945. More than 1,300 Mariners were built, and their service life lasted 16 years. *US Navy, courtesy Stan Piet*

we could collect or improvise. The enlisted complement was also less than half of normal, and only half that *number reached Guadalcanal until 232 was past the peak of its contribution. Under the circumstances, and in light of later experience, it was rather remarkable that our contribution was effective.*

I might observe that all this was pretty good testimony not only to the sort of planning that went on in the early part of the war, but also to the long calculated risks the high command accepted in committing US forces to stopping the Japanese at Guadalcanal. That it all worked seems remarkable to me yet!

A few days prior to launch from the Long Island (CVE-1), *we received radio orders to hang a 500-pound bomb on each SBD because the supply at Guadalcanal was so meager. Consternation! We could see ourselves flopping into the water off*

the bow! On 20 August, however, the wind came up and we had some 30 knots over the deck. Launching was no problem.

We had no information whatever about Guadalcanal. To be sure, the general concept of Marine Corps operations and training envisions rough field conditions—just how rough sometimes seems a bit shocking even to Marines!

There were no vehicles for fueling and arming, thus these functions were tedious and time consuming. Ordnance and fuel drums had to be manhandled, and there wasn't any manpower. Fuel was hand pumped from drums and the pumps quickly wore out. Fatigue of personnel, plus lack of adequate food or rest, made for a descending spiral which accounted, with losses incident to operations, for the relatively short sojourn of the first units in the Battle for Guadalcanal.

For about two days there was practically no maintenance done. We just flew 'em as they were. The SBD bomb release was mechanical—yank a lever connected by wire to the bomb release. In an attack on a Japanese ship on 25 August I wasn't able to drop so I climbed up and went back to try again. Dirt in the works may have contributed or maybe I simply didn't yank hard enough. At any rate, it released all right when I went back with it.

There was no aerial opposition for all practical purposes. There were enough clouds to lurk behind in those pre-radar days. I did find myself suddenly face to face with a Japanese single-engine floatplane and had a good shot at him but the synchronized guns, which never worked very well, sometimes didn't work at all. We both sought the interior of friendly clouds and I never saw him again.

Marine Air Group 23 was by mid-September pretty much a collection of remnants. I had lost most of my pilots, some through combat, some from night shelling, some from accidents. Two or three of us left did some flying after mid-September, but in the main the fresh new units carried the load.

At war's end Mangrum was a colonel commanding MAG-45 in Ulithi. Universally respected as a leader, he retired as assistant commandant of the Marine Corps and lived in North Carolina until his death.

In a rare attempt at interservice cooperation, the Japanese Army and Navy came back in strength in late October. The result was the Battle of Santa Cruz, with four Japanese carriers ranged against *Enterprise* and *Hornet*. Two enemy flattops were damaged but "The Big E" was badly hit and *Hornet* was sunk. *Enterprise* also might have been lost except for the superb performance by Lieutenant Stanley W. Vejtasa.

A former SBD pilot, "Swede" Vejtasa joined VF-10 at Flatley's invitation and became the right man in the right place at the right time. With successive waves of Japanese dive bombers and torpedo planes attacking Task Force 61, the Montana native was credited with seven confirmed kills—at that time an American record. With ammo expended and fumes in his tanks, he got aboard *Enterprise* thanks to the gifted landing signal officer, Lieutenant Robin Lindsey. It was a close-run thing: the flight deck was holed forward of the stern, so Lindsey skillfully "cut" Vejtasa into the number-one arresting wire.

During the four carrier battles of 1942, the US Navy lost three carriers and the Japanese six. Additionally, *Wasp* was sunk by a submarine in mid-September, and another Japanese sub put *Saratoga* out of commission in late August. Clearly, the US Navy needed more fleet carriers.

Experienced aviators also were in short supply during 1942. The same names appeared repeatedly in the after-action reports, and estimates show that approximately 400 Navy pilots bore the brunt of carrier combat in the crucial period from Pearl Harbor to Guadalcanal. Not until the expanded flight training program took effect in 1943 could those few hundred fliers expect relief.

Midway and Guadalcanal determined that the Pacific War would become a prolonged conflict of attrition—the type of

Aviation ordnancemen load bombs aboard an early model Lockheed PV-1 Ventura in the Aleutians. Red surround on national insignia indicates the photo was taken during summer 1943. The aircraft markings also indicate the Ventura was assigned to VPB-135, the Navy's intial PV squadron, during its first combat tour. *US Navy, courtesy Stan Piet*

The ruins of war are seen in this November 1945 photo of Japanese aircraft at Atsugi Airfield, Japan. Aircraft include Mitsubishi A6M5 Zeke and J2M3 Jack fighters, with Nakajima J1N1 Irving recon planes. *USAF*

Left
Following trouble-plagued initial fleet service attempts with Air Groups Nine and Ten, Curtiss SB2C-1 Helldivers finally became operational with VB-17 on board *Bunker Hill* (CV-17). VB-4 and -6 SB2C-1s prepare for launch from the new *Yorktown* (CV-10) in mid-1943, during her Atlantic Fleet shakedown cruise. *US Navy, courtesy Richard M. Hill*

business, some of which explored the boundaries of human courage.

PatRon 34 was a PBY-5A unit which flew frequent Dumbo missions. On 15 February 1944, Lieutenant Nathan Gordon was circling nearby while Army A-20 Havocs and B-25 Mitchells struck Kavieng Harbor, New Britain. Three of the twin-engine bombers were shot down in the harbor, and the P-47 Thunderbolt escort called in Gordon to attempt a rescue.

Despite intense antiaircraft and smallarms fire, Gordon landed near the first raft he saw. Taxiing close, he found it was empty and took off. But soon six bomber crewmen were spotted in another rubber raft and the Cat splashed down nearby. However, Gordon's crew reported that the Army men had trouble getting aboard; the idling engine tended to blow the raft

Buchanan (DD-484) refuels from *Wasp* (CV-7) during an August 1942 underway replenishment period in the Solomons. The ability of US Navy task forces to replenish underway was a vital asset in conducting the war throughout the far reaches of the Pacific. *LTJG John R. Prann, US Navy, courtesy T.J. Wilkes*

away from the aircraft. Gordon shut down to ease the transfer, still under fire from shore. He then restarted, turned about, and took off into heavy swells.

A third landing was accomplished to rescue three more men, but the PBY had sprung serious leaks. Headed home with nine survivors and considerable water aboard, Gordon was notified that yet another raft had been sighted by the P-47s. He wheeled about and headed back, willing to risk nineteen lives (including his own crew) to save another six.

This landing was the wildest of the day. Gordon had to fly his approach directly over the beach at low level in order to reach the Army men. He landed a mere 600 yards from shore, fully exposed to automatic weapons fire. Somehow he got the final half-dozen fliers aboard and managed an overloaded take-off with twenty-five men in the crowded PBY.

Nathan Gordon became only the fifth Navy pilot awarded the Medal of Honor in World War II. No other decoration was thinkable.

This image printed from a 16mm motion picture frame is the only known color photo of *Arizona* (BB-39) exploding during the Japanese attack on Pearl Harbor 7 Dec 1941. Six carriers launched 383 sorties against America's military complex on Oahu, killing more than 2,000 servicemen and civilians while virtually destroying the Pacific Fleet's battle line and Army Air Corps power in the Pacific. At sea during the attack, the carriers were spared to become the country's first offensive weapons against the Japanese. *US Navy, courtesy Don S. Montgomery*

NAS Kaneohe, T.H., personnel honor dead comrades killed in the 7 Dec 1941 attack. Kaneohe, located on the northeast side of Oahu, was the first and hardest hit military installation struck by the Japanese carrier aircraft. *US Navy, courtesy Russ Egnor*

Dumbo crews continued such heroics almost to war's end. Little more than a year later another Catalina found itself in similar circumstances. Seventh Air Force P-51 Mustangs from newly won Iwo Jima flew frequent strikes against other islands in the Bonins. A Mustang pilot had bailed out near Chichi Jima and was reported immobile in his raft. The duty Dumbo landed offshore and moved in close while under mortar and machine gun fire. The Army pilot remained unmoving, but rather than abandon him the Catalina crew put a man into the raft to confirm the flier was dead. Only then did the flying boat depart.

That episode, while resulting in no rescue, required a particular brand of courage. The Catalina crew risked more than death, for Chichi Jima was occupied by fanatical Japanese under a barbarian commander, later executed for war crimes which included ceremonial beheadings and cannibalism of captured American fliers.

Two other flying boats served in the Pacific, including Consolidated's follow-on, the PB2Y Coronado. A huge four-engine aircraft with a 115-foot wingspan and gross weight of 68,000 pounds, the Coronado first flew in 1937. Because of the extravagant price of $300,000 (three times a PBY), only 176 PB2Y-3s were built. They experienced little combat, but remained in service to the end of 1945. The last 41 were built exclusively as transports in the PB2Y-2R variant, raising total production to barely 220.

Martin's gull-winged PBM Mariner was more numerous and generally more successful. The twin-engine, twin-tailed PBM first flew in 1939 and joined the fleet in fall of 1940. Its gross weight fell five tons below the Coronado's but lacked the PB2Y's speed. However, a one-ton ordnance load was possible, and the PBM-3C and -3D variants carried radar primarily for antisubmarine patrol. More than 1,300 Mariners were built, and their service life lasted sixteen years.

Among land-based naval aircraft, two main types dominated. Lockheed's PV series began with navalized Venturas, including 380 taken from lend-lease shipments to Britain. Some 1,600 PV-1s were delivered from late 1943 to mid-1944, and they served well. Exceptionally fast and well armed, they boasted six .50-cal. machine guns. Equipped with six depth charges or bombs, PV-1s could find their prey in darkness or poor weather with airborne radar. In fact, a Marine Corps squadron became the naval service's first night-fighter unit with PV-1s, flying in the Solomons during 1943.

The bigger PV-2 Harpoon was ordered in June 1943. With almost ten feet more wingspan and a half ton heavier, its top speed was lower than the PV-1 but cruise was marginally

Credit for being the first squadron to take the Hellcat into combat goes to LCDR Jimmy Flatley's VF-5 when they launched from *Yorktown* (CV-10) on 31 Aug 1943 for strikes against Marcus Is. CAG 5 Flatley awaits start signal during the Marcus strikes. *US Navy/LT Charles R. Kerlee*

another five seconds under water. As it turned out, I was flying again the next day. An attempt to salvage the airplane was abandoned since it went down in something like 1,000 fathoms.

By late August 1943, we had eight Corsair squadrons in the Solomons, and additional Army fighters—P-40s and P-38s. So we had enough planes to put up a good show and escort the bombers.

On the 30th I got in one of the worst battles I ever was in. We were escorting B-24s to Kahili when I had engine trouble again. My supercharger quit and I had to turn back. I remembered the advance strip at Munda and headed there.

Another Marine ace, Lieutenant Roger Conant of VMF-215, later accused me of stealing his airplane. I landed at Munda and saw an old friend, Major Jim Neefus, who was in charge of the field. I told him that I wanted to catch up with my squadron but I needed a plane. He drove me to the flight line in his jeep and said, "Take your pick." So I jumped in the closest one and took off. Forty-five years later I met Roger Conant who told me he watched this stranger climb into his F4U and take off—and didn't bring it back!

I knew that the B-24s would overfly Kahili and turn for their bomb run from the southeast. By cutting the corners I caught up with them just as a flock of about 50 Zeros hit them over Bougainville. I was alone, but I jumped in and was able to shoot down two of them within a couple miles of each other.

About 70 miles southeast of the target I tangled with another bunch of Zeros and got two more. There was a very active few minutes there. I was covering some B-24s at low altitude, making a descent coming out of Kahili, and we lost one of the bombers. I saw a bomber hit bad, then go in; no survivors.

I got badly shot up by four more Zeros that had me boxed in. I was trying to get away at low level and ran out of altitude to bail out so I had to put it in the water. My engine was hit, and though I tried to make it back to Munda, I had to put down off Vella Lavella. I laugh when I say that I knew how to do it, because I'd done it before, on 1 February.

Anyway, a Higgins boat came out and picked me up, along with a P-39 pilot. I'd seen him go down. Evidently he was on CAP near Vella Lavella and saw the action going on. He joined the fracas though he didn't have the range to go where we did, and he didn't have the performance to tangle with the Zero in the first place.

Eastern Aircraft-built FM-2 Wildcats of VC-83 during catapult launch from *Makin Island* (CVE-93) for a February 1945 strike against Iwo Jima. FM-2s operated from escort carriers until the end of the war. The last F4F Wildcat carrier squadron in Pacific combat was VC-33 in *Anzio* (CVE-57), flying -4s until September 1944. *US Navy, courtesy Don S. Montgomery*

But he got into the action and got where he shouldn't be. His name was Lieutenant Fowler. The first thing he experienced was a 20mm through his canopy and into his instrument panel. His plane caught fire, and miraculously he was able to bail out but he broke his leg when he hit the stabilizer.

Pilots receive prestrike briefing in one of *Lexington's* (CV-16) ready rooms c. 1943–44. *US Navy, courtesy Russ Egnor*

He landed near the island of Gizo and some friendly natives picked him up in a canoe. They rowed him over to Vella Lavella where I was, and we were in sick bay together. He wanted to know what was going on, and I asked, "What happened to you?" When I found out he was in a P-39 I said, "Well, I saw you get hit and go in."

The next day they put us on an LST and sent us back to Guadalcanal.

Walsh finished his Solomons tour with 20 confirmed victories. Awarded the Medal of Honor for missions on 15 and 30 August, he returned to combat at Okinawa and shot down one more Japanese aircraft. During the Korean War he commanded a transport squadron and retired as a lieutenant colonel.

The Central Pacific offensive began with strikes against Marcus Island on 31 August 1943. The standard tactical organization was the task group, usually two CVs and two CVLs with cruiser and destroyer screens, frequently augmented with fast

Positioning and movement of aircraft on board carriers is a precision process planned and tracked in the aircraft handler's spaces, located at the base of the island at flight deck level. *Randolph* (CV-15) crewman keeps aircraft positions up to date by use of made-to-scale templates on a metal board outline of the flight and hangar decks. *US Navy, courtesy Don S. Montgomery*

Right
Flight deck maintenance crew works on a VT-5 TBF-1 Avenger on board *Yorktown* (CV-10) in late 1943. *US Navy, courtesy Russ Egnor*

VF-16 CO LCDR Paul D. Buie, "briefs" his pilots in staged photo on flight deck of *Lexington* (CV-16) during the November-December 1943 Gilberts Is. operations. By the end of the war, Fighting 16 pilots were credited with 154 aerial victories, 18 probables and 12 on the ground. *US Navy/CDR Edw. Steichen, courtesy Russ Egnor*

battleships for additional antiaircraft gunfire. It was a curious reversal of prewar doctrine in which carriers were most often regarded as secondary to the battle line.

The Fast Carrier Task Force was composed of four task groups under overall command of a vice admiral. Depending upon the fleet commander (Halsey with Third Fleet or Spruance with Fifth Fleet), the carrier striking arm was designated Task Force 38 or Task Force 58. The designation changed whenever the fleet command alternated for planning purposes. This system allowed one team to conduct an operation while the other prepared for the next. It also helped confuse the Japanese.

When instituted in January 1944, the Fast Carrier Task Force was commanded by Marc A. Mitscher. He remained in command, alternating the TF-38/58 designation with John S. McCain, until that fall. Mitscher was Naval Aviator Number 33, a veteran flier who had won his wings in 1916. He commanded *Hornet* during the Doolittle raid and Midway, then became Commander Aircraft, Solomons.

In contrast, "Slew" McCain came late to aviation, passing through Pensacola in 1936. Like King and Halsey, he had more seniority than most "real" aviators at a time when rank was needed in the growing world of naval aviation.

The task group commanders were rear admirals, nearly all of whom had spent most of their careers in aviation. They were the original flying admirals, men who had personally tested early carrier aircraft, designed and perfected shipboard equipment, and evolved the tactics of dive-bombing and torpedo attack. They included aviation true believers and longtime aviators such as Jerry Bogan, Jocko Clark, Dave Davison, and Arthur Radford.

Though Americans knew the names of admirals and aces, precious little attention was given to enlisted aircrewmen. Sadly, it was not a situation limited to the public; it existed within the Navy as well.

The Guys in the Back

James M. Geyton flew as a radioman-gunner from *Enterprise* for three years. His perspective as a combat air crewman speaks for thousands of anonymous young men, many of whom never grew old.

When I came aboard in 1941, radiomen and gunners in the SBD and TBD squadrons were much older than us newcomers, and the majority were rough and tough. They were also extremely helpful and took the time to teach us the trade. I remember one such individual, ARM3/c Godfrey. He let me assist him in making up some antennas for his SBD. I made mis-

CVLG-30 aircraft prepare raid on the Gilberts Is. during November–December 1943 on board *Monterey* (CVL-26). Nine light carriers were converted from cruiser hulls under construction in 1943. Their speed allowed them to join the larger Essex-class CVs to become part of the Fast Carrier Task Force of WWII. *US Navy*

Somewhat rusty and worn, *Sangamon* (CVE-26), with CVEG-37 embarked, rests at anchor in an unidentified harbor sometime in 1943. The lightly armored escort carriers were given the appellation: Combustible, Vulnerable, and Expendable. *US Navy, courtesy Russ Egnor*

takes but he straightened me out. I had my first flight wearing his gear. He was six feet-plus tall; I am five and a half feet tall. His flight jacket wrapped around me and the earphones were at my cheekbone level.

During 1942 many aircrewmen flew combat missions at Coral Sea, Midway, and Guadalcanal. Many pilots received Navy Crosses, and they deserved every one of them. There was a great reluctance to nominate any enlisted person for a decoration of any type, however, unless it was posthumously! COs such as Joe Clifton, Bill Martin, and others tried, but the battleship admirals were not recommending any enlisted personnel. In those days, a DFC would earn you $5 a month extra.

By 1943, these battleship admirals had been replaced by aviation-minded senior officers, such as McCain, Mitscher, Halsey, and even Spruance.

As reserve officers came into the squadrons they began to question, "What about my crew? We are a team and survived together. Don't they deserve recognition?"

In VT-10, Commander (later Vice Admiral) William I. Martin saw to it our work was recognized. There still were some diehards, but the dam had broken and enlisted crewmen began to be recognized and rewarded.

On 1 April 1944 (commenting on a VB-10 crew that had been killed at Palau), Lieutenant Jerry Flynn made an announcement regarding the loss of Lieu-

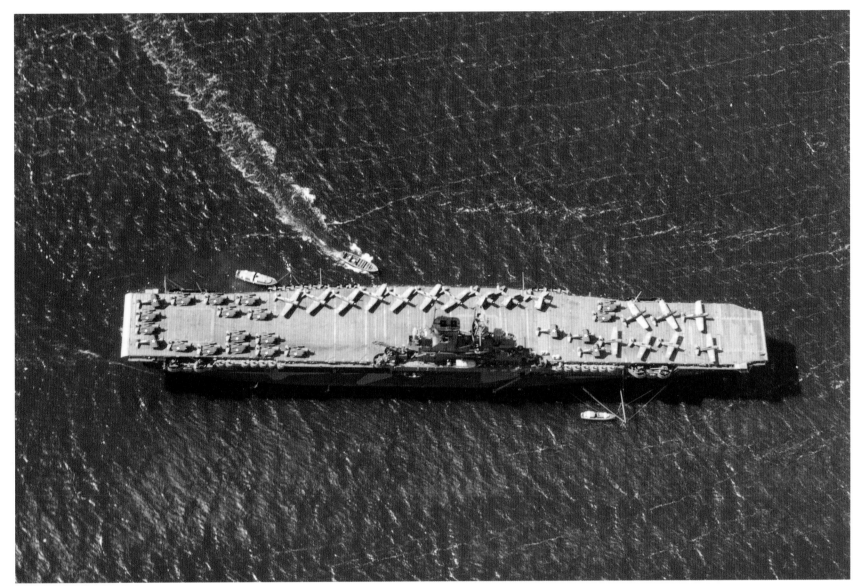

Still carrying Douglas TBD-1 Devastators and Vought SB2U-2 Vindicators, *Wasp* (CV-7) is at anchor in San Diego, California during June 1942. The prewar types were soon traded for Grumman TBF-1 Avengers and Douglas SBD-3 Dauntlesses, which she carried into the Pacific war. *US Navy, courtesy Don S. Montgomery*

placed my gunsight pipper on the center of the aircraft and squeezed the trigger. The aircraft exploded instantly.

Skidding over to the center Val, I was about 50 feet from him. The rear gunner was trying to unsecure his gun. I placed the pipper on his chest. Squeezing the trigger, the vertical stabilizer disintegrated and a couple of bullets hit him in the body. The aircraft exploded in the right wingroot.

By this time I was moving behind the third plane; my speed was hard to control. The gunner had unsecured his gun and was firing directly at me. I did not know if I was taking hits. I remember holding down the trigger, firing at this plane, because he did not want to burn. I remember saying, "Burn,

you bastard." If he had not exploded, I am afraid I would have collided with him because I was too close to turn away.

After these first three Vals, I raised my landing gear and moved behind another three-plane division. I placed my pipper on the gunner who was also firing at me, no more than 60 feet away. I could see the color of his flight suit, helmet, and skin. He seemed to give up. He took his hands off his gun and put them in front of his face—maybe he thought I was going to ram him. Several .50 cal. slugs hit him in the face.

They say that killing for a fighter pilot is not personal, but don't you believe it. The aircraft started burning and the pilot bailed out at less than 200 feet.

One of only three prewar carriers that would survive WWII, *Saratoga* (CV-3) is moored at Ford Island in Pearl Harbor during early 1942. Sara was sunk during the 1946 Operation Crossroads atom bomb tests at Bikini. *US Navy, courtesy Don S. Montgomery*

Design of the Grumman F8F-1 Bearcat was begun in 1943, but the aircraft, which may have been the finest piston-engined fighter to ever fly, did not reach the fleet in time for WWII combat. By the time of the Korean War, it was already being replaced in the fleet and its only combat would come with the French and Vietnamese in Indochina. This F8F-1 was assigned to Pax River's Armament Test Division in November 1946. *Fred Bamberger*

The next plane in the middle got away, but I managed to get behind the one on the right. He started shedding pieces and smoking badly, then the tail disintegrated and the plane flamed and fell.

By this time there were planes all over the sky. Bill Blair's division and Russ Reiserer's night fighters, both from Hornet, had arrived. This is what saved me. No matter where you looked, you could see a parachute or a burning plane. It was like a movie of a flying circus, but this was real. Every time you saw an explosion, someone died.

After downing my fifth plane, my guns stopped firing and I headed away from the fight. By kicking my gun chargers I got two guns working again, one on each side, and headed back into the fight.

I saw a Val coming toward me, about 1,000 feet high. I got him in my sight and squeezed the trigger. As the two guns fired, another started firing also. The plane flashed and exploded. It came apart just behind the pilot. My guns quit again so I headed out until I managed to get three guns working.

As I turned back into the fight, I saw another Val low over the water. I nosed over to intercept and started firing. I killed the gunner as the plane flashed and started burning. We were then about 75 feet over the water. I had to pull up to avoid the cliffs and did not see the plane crash, but there was no place for him to go. He had to have hit the cliffs.

My guns stopped again after the last burst. Kicking the hell out of my chargers again, one gun started. I spotted one of our Hellcats in trouble. He was only about 100 feet over the water. He had two Zeros on him; he was in a bad way with his landing gear down. I only had one gun but I shed a few pieces off one Zero, running them off. The Hellcat pilot was Bill Leverings, one of the night fighters.

By this time all Japanese formations had separated in utter confusion. A Val had just turned on base leg to land on the bombed runways. I whipped around at about 200 feet. As I squeezed the trigger the aircraft belched flame and black smoke. The aircraft started a violent roll to the right and crashed in the rocks.

My last attempt to get another aircraft was on a Zero. He was making a final turn to land on the bombed-out strip and I only had two guns working. He started to burn but nosed into the water about 100 yards offshore.

Finally my guns were all inoperative and I headed out to the open sea, where a VF-2 Hellcat joined me. I was sure glad to see Jack Vaughn. He signaled me to ask how many planes I had shot down. I signaled eight. He indicated that he had three. I gave him the lead and signaled that my radio was out and for him to take us home.

Aboard *Hornet*, Webb's Hellcat was so badly damaged that it was pushed overboard. Because of a defective gun camera, he was credited with six confirmed kills and two probables in his first combat. He retired as a commander and began a second career in the aviation industry.

American aircraft losses on 19 June amounted to fewer than 30, of which 16 were Hellcats lost in combat. While a handful of Japanese bombers got through the efficient CAP, no significant damage was inflicted on any of Mitscher's ships. Meanwhile, US submarines found Ozawa and torpedoed his flagship, *Taiho*, and a Pearl Harbor veteran, *Shokaku*. Both went to the bottom.

Search aircraft located the beaten Japanese force fleeing westward the next afternoon. Mitscher calculated the odds of retrieving some 220 planes in darkness, as the enemy Mobile Fleet steamed 300 miles away. Few TF 58 air groups were qualified in night landings, but after pondering a moment, Mitscher decided to go. Turning to his staff on *Lexington's* bridge, he merely said, "Launch 'em."

It was a long flight into the westering sun that evening, and darkness was approaching as the strike groups deployed to attack. The priority targets were enemy carriers, as none had been brought to battle in 20 months. Owing to diminishing fuel, *Wasp's* (CV-18) planes went after the enemy oilers, the first ships sighted. But everybody was short of gasoline, and the other groups tackled what *Enterprise's* VB-10 skipper Lieutenant Commander James D. Ramage called "the fighting navy."

The results were disappointing. Intense enemy flak and limited but aggressive fighter cover reduced the effectiveness of the strike, and only one carrier was sunk. VT-24 off *Belleau Wood* (CVL-24) launched a four-plane division which selected *Hiyo*. Three of the TBM pilots completed their runs, probably scoring two hits. The division leader was Lieutenant (jg) George Brown, an exceptionally courageous flier who had promised his skipper to get a flattop. And he did, but his Avenger was so badly damaged that he ordered his crew to bail out. They were recovered the next day, but Brown flew into the dark and never returned.

About 20 TF 58 planes were lost over the target, but nearly 200 had to find their carriers in total darkness. Many ran out of fuel and others simply became lost. When nearing the recovery point, however, the aviators were astonished to see a myriad of lights showing the way. Ignoring the submarine threat, "Pete" Mitscher had decided to risk all for his fliers. The lights, however, proved both a blessing and a bane. With every TF 58 ship running its truck lights or more, the result was confusion to tired, frightened aviators. Alex Vraciu, returning to *Lexington* after making his nineteenth kill, could hardly believe the

Curtiss SC-1 Seahawks were the last scoutplanes built for the Navy and began replacing its predecessors in October 1944. The last SCs were assigned to HU-2 in October 1949, ending the era of scout floatplanes in the US Navy. Utility Squadron Seven SC-1 taxis onto the recovery mat while assigned to *Alaska* (CB-1) during 6 Mar 1945 operations off Iwo Jima. Pilot is LT Jess A. Faulconer, Jr., USNR. *US Navy, courtesy Don S. Montgomery*

sight. The depth of his gratitude was evident years later when he named a son after Admiral Mitscher.

When it was over, nearly half of the 216 planes on the mission were lost. Fuel starvation was the main cause, and SB2C squadrons were especially hard hit. Supposedly longer ranged than the SBD it replaced, the Helldiver made a miserable showing that night: of 50 launched, only five were back aboard the next morning. Later, with more experience and upgraded models, SB2C pilots coaxed more range from their bombers.

Whatever disappointment existed over the mission, there was room for cheer in the next two days: 77 percent of

Above and next page

The Marines returned to carrier aviation in December 1944 by augmenting Navy Essex-class CVGs with fighter support to counter the new *kamikaze* threat. In October 1944, 18 Marine carrier air groups were authorized (only seven or eight were formed) to operate from new Commencement-class (CVE-109) escort carriers soon to join the fleet. Beginning CVE operations in February 1945, the MCVGs participated in combat operations at Okinawa and against the Japanese homeland. At left, catapult crew hooks up VMTB-132 TBM-3E Avenger for launch from *Cape Gloucester* (CVE-109) during 8 Sep 1945 operations off Kyushu, Japan. At right, -132 TBM recovers aboard the same day. *USMC, courtesy Robert J. Cressman*

the downed fliers were recovered in an unusually efficient rescue operation.

The greater implication of the Marianas campaign became evident by year's end, as General Curtis LeMay's XX Bomber Command began flying very long range (VLR) missions from Guam, Saipan, and Tinian. As ever-growing numbers of Boeing B-29s arrived, the Superfortresses brought war to the Japanese government and people with cataclysmic finality.

Subsequent operations over the Marianas and the Bonins (primarily Iwo Jima) further enhanced American air superiority.

Large, violent dogfights continued in these arenas for a short time as the eager F6F pilots sought to emulate the "turkey shoot" of 19 June. But following occupation of the Palaus in August, only 500 miles from the Philippines, even greater opportunities arose.

One of the Pacific Fleet's continuing logistic problems was maintaining sufficient aircraft aboard forward-deployed carriers. The concern had been heightened with onset of the Marianas campaign in June 1944, as AirPac planners recognized the need for a large afloat pool of replacement aircraft to offset combat and operational attrition.

Groundwork was laid in the spring, as transport escort carriers—CVE(T)s—were placed under Carrier Transport Squadron Pacific effective 1 June. Operationally, CVE(T)s served under Third/Fifth Fleet refueling groups and later with an independent at-sea replenishment group.

Previously a CVE had been delegated as replenishment carrier for specific operations such as the two-day Truk raid in February 1944. But in the Marianas—the most ambitious amphibious operation undertaken to that time—an entire task group was formed for the purpose. Captain E.E. Pare' headed the fueling group, comprised of 24 fleet oilers and four CVEs.

By the end of 1944, the At-Sea Logistics Group numbered eight CVEs, 29 oilers, eight ammunition ships, and 36 escorts.

Another unglamorous task continued unabated in the Central Pacific. Since America's island-hopping strategy required bypassing many Japanese garrisons, the pressure had to be maintained against enemy-held atolls in the backwater of the war. Much of that chore fell to the Fourth Marine Aircraft Wing, based throughout the Marshalls and Gilberts.

By early 1944, the wing's four squadrons were flying from Kwajalein Atoll, perennially bombing Japanese bases at Wotje, Maloelap, Mili, and Jaluit. Flying Dauntlesses, Helldivers, and Corsairs, the leathernecks became extremely proficient dive bombers. They continued their unheralded but necessary work until the end of the war.

A planning conference that summer had determined the course of American strategy in the Pacific. Rather than advancing through Formosa and along the China coast, as the Navy preferred, Admirals King and Nimitz acceded to the Army. Partly to restore American credibility in Asia, partly to sate General Douglas MacArthur's ego, the decision was made to return to the Philippines.

The multifaceted Battle of Leyte Gulf in October was also called Second Philippine Sea. But whatever the name, it finished Japan as a naval power. In the Sibuyan Sea, on the west side of the Philippines, carrier air destroyed one of the largest battleships afloat on 24 October. Multiple strikes against Vice Admiral Takeo Kurita's surface force put the 64,000-ton battleship *Musashi* under, in large part due to an Air Group 20 attack led by Commander Dan F. Smith.

Sinking Musashi

Lieutenant Commander Joseph T. Lawler was a former floatplane pilot when he became executive officer of VF-20 in October 1943. A year later he led the Hellcat escort for the *Enterprise* strike against the major Japanese surface force in one of the most important missions flown against battleships in World War II.

At 1315 on 24 October 1944, Enterprise launched 38 aircraft for an attack on Japanese warships in the Sibuyan Sea. This force was one of three divisions of the Japanese fleet sent to provoke a final showdown with the US Navy. This 150-mile carrier strike was led by Commander Dan Smith, CAG 20. I was one of the type flight leaders with 16 F6F-5s, each plane carrying six five-inch rockets. The bomber flight leader of 14 SB2Cs, loaded with 1,000-pound bombs, was Lieutenant Jim Cooper. The torpedo flight leader of eight TBMs was Lieutenant Commander Sam Prickett, with each Avenger carrying a torpedo.

A running rendezvous was made en route to the target with a gradual climb so that the base element (VT) was at about 12,000 feet. After passing over Samar Island and flying into the Sibuyan Sea, the enemy force was sighted. First noticeable were the distinct white wakes of the ships in the blue water. With CAVU conditions, except for some small cumulus, and with little wind,

Assigned to MCVG-4, VMF-351 provided fighter cover and flew bombing missions from *Cape Gloucester* (CVE-109) during the Okinawa campaign and attacks against the Japanese home islands. Vought F4U-1D Corsair is readied for launch 8 Sep 1945. *USMC, courtesy Robert J. Cressman*

the wakes were very visible for 20 to 30 miles. When first sighted, the enemy fleet was in a cruising disposition, circular screen, on course 090, at about 20 knots. This fleet consisted of two task groups, one ahead of the other, separated by several miles. The flight coordinator, CAG 20, designated one the west group, the other the east group.

The west group consisted of three battleships, four cruisers, and seven or eight destroyers. The east group consisted of two battleships, four cruisers, and six destroyers. At this time, Japan had the two largest battleships in the world, estimated to be 42,000 tons (later determined to be 64,000 tons) carrying 18-inch guns. One of the battleships in the west group was one of these monstrous twins. The flight coordinator designated the west group as our target, with the large battleship as the main objective.

The strike group flew a westerly heading and passed south of both enemy task groups. When still 15 miles away at about 12,000 feet, the enemy opened fire with the main battery. Though very inaccurate, these bursts were tremendous and very spectacular with colors of purple, red, blue, yellow, and white. Some bursts contained double-bursting streamers.

The strike group continued west until passing the west group of enemy ships, then turned north to get up sun. At this time, all enemy ships turned right 180 degrees except the large

battleship, a cruiser, and a destroyer, which made a 180 to the left. This gave a separation between the large battleship and the rest of the formation. The air coordinator assigned all VB and VT to the northernmost ship, the large battleship. The VF were assigned the cruiser and the destroyer.

Approach was made on a northeast course. Some ten miles out, the VT turned left 045 degrees and started a high-speed letdown. The VF turned right 045 degrees at the same time and began their high-speed letdown. The VB continued on course and altitude toward the pushover point. This procedure separated the strike group into three separate units and therefore divided the antiaircraft fire. After widely separating, the VF turned left toward their target, and the VT turned right toward theirs. As a result, a simultaneous coordinated attack was made from three different directions. The VB were attacking from overhead, the VF from the southeast and the VT from the southwest. As the attack continued, all enemy ships opened up with intense antiaircraft fire.

As each squadron separated from the air group to proceed independently for a simultaneous attack, I had an opportunity to look down and digest what a formidable array of enemy ships was below us. Except for lack of aircraft carriers, each of the two Japanese groups looked like one of our own. I knew the tremendous volume of AA fire a task group like this could throw at us. I also knew that even after months of combat, we had never attacked a target as tough as this one would be.

As we approached our pushover point, I announced to the other fighter divisions not to attack the battleship, but to pick out a support ship for attack close aboard the BB. Our armament would have little effect on a battleship but might have some effect on topside personnel on a smaller ship. I picked a cruiser as my division's target.

From about 17,000 feet we pushed over rapidly and settled in about a 60-degree dive. As soon as I could get the pipper on the cruiser, I opened fire with six guns, firing short bursts all the way down. At about 3,500 feet the ship looked big in the gunsight, and after a long and steady pipper I salvoed six HVAR rockets. I could see some people topside manning light, exposed AA guns, all shooting like crazy. At our airspeed the rockets went straight and true. A slow, gradual pullout was made to the north at low altitude and maximum speed.

Rendezvous with the strike group was made about 20 miles north. The large battleship—later identified as Musashi—was hit with 8 torpedoes and 10 to 12 bombs. The cruiser was severely damaged by rocket fire, and the rocket hits on the destroyer apparently hit depth charges or torpedoes on deck, since a violent explosion resulted. The air coordina-

Aleutian-based Consolidated PatWing Four PBY-5A Catalina and Lockheed PV-1 Venturas at rest between missions during summer 1943. PVs are assigned to either VB-135, or -136. *US Navy*

tor remained in the vicinity while the remainder of the strike group started to return to base. When seen 30 minutes after attack, the battleship was dead in the water so far down by the bow that the forecastle was awash. All aircraft returned to Enterprise *about 1730.*

Later, Carrier Air Group Twenty was given major credit for sinking Musashi *and the destroyer, which had exploded.*

Lawler remained in the Navy, commanded an air group, and retired as a captain. He settled in Coronado, California.

Kurita's powerful battleship and surface force was turned back, but during that night reversed course and headed for San Bernardino Strait. The object was MacArthur's amphibious force in Leyte Gulf which, if attacked by Kurita's big-gun ships, stood

After its aborted prewar XF5F-1 attempt at a twin-engine fighter, Grumman was more successful with its F7F Tigercat. Primarily used by the Marines—not used in combat by the Navy or with its carrier squadrons—the Tigercat first reported to VMF-911, a Marine replacement training squadron, in January 1944, and VMF(N)-531 received F7F-1N night fighters soon thereafter. CAPT Sheldon O. Hall, USMC, credited with six aerial victories while flying F4Us with VMF-213, poses on the wing of F7F-2N at Grumman's Bethpage, N.Y., plant in 1946. *Courtesy CAPT W.E. Scarborough, USN (Ret)*

little chance of survival. A typically complex Japanese plan involved Ozawa's four remaining carriers well to the north and another surface unit to the south. Admiral Halsey was correctly assessed by the Japanese as being unable to resist the decoy flat-tops and took his fast carriers north, leaving the gulf vulnerable.

The southern force was annihilated in a nocturnal surface battle, but Kurita emerged into the gulf shortly past dawn on 25 October. All that stood in his way was an escort carrier unit composed of six CVEs and their seven escorts. This small group, code-named "Taffy Three," took on four battleships, eight cruisers, and eleven destroyers.

Battle Off Samar

Commanding VC-10 aboard *Gambier Bay* (CVE-73) was Lieutenant Commander Edward J. Huxtable. Like most Taffy Three personnel, he did not immediately realize the CVEs' dreadful peril.

I got in my TBM and asked Jerry Gutzweiler, my plane captain, if I had a bomb load. He said no, so I told him to call Buzz Borries, the air officer, if I had time to get a load. We had not turned up the engines as yet, and I couldn't see any use going off without some ordnance.

About this time, I was startled by what seemed a rifle shot next to my left ear. I looked and saw that it was a salvo of heavy-caliber stuff splashing alongside the White Plains. Until this moment I had no idea the enemy was so near. Now I was more than ready to get on that catapult. We turned up engines and three TBMs launched ahead of me. As I shot off, the lead plane had started his 180-degree turn for a regular carrier joinup. The ceiling was low at about 1,200 feet. After I took the lead I called Admiral Sprague's code name, Bendix, and asked what our orders were. They came back in an excited voice: "Attack immediately."

We were headed aft with relation to the ship, and the visibility being poor, I could just see the destroyer plane guards. We shortly broke out into better visibility and higher ceilings, where I spotted four cruisers near and what appeared to be four battleships farther back in the gloom. There was no possibility of making a high-altitude attack, so I turned back over the destroyers and our carriers, and turned on a course I figured would bring us out over the Jap cruisers. I pulled up into the ceiling and started for the cruisers. What loads the other planes had I did not know, but at least we would give the Japs a scare.

Suddenly we broke into the clear again on the starboard side of the cruisers. I broke left and started for the after cruiser in a shallow dive, doing about 190 knots. The other planes had picked their own targets. When I got within 3,000 yards, the AA fire was getting too hot and I couldn't see being a hero without a bomb load, so I turned left and pulled out aft. I made a wide circle, passing ahead of the cruiser column, and came in on their starboard side, paralleling them and watching for their next move.

I thought I was far enough out at 3,000 to 4,000 yards so they wouldn't shoot at me. Then the different colored 5in bursts appeared about 150 yards in front of me and I ran through the smoke of the middle burst.

About this time I called Bendix and suggested that his best course was south. I came back over the carriers and called Gambier Bay. The ship answered and suggested that we go to Tacloban to arm and refuel. But I doubted they had anything there, and I thought we could do more good just harassing the Japanese. The carriers had come into the clear again, and at this time Bill Gallagher joined me with his engine smoking. He had launched after I did and made a torpedo attack. I told him to head for the beach and he turned off. Another pilot reported that he saw Bill make a water landing, but Bill and his crew were never recovered.

After returning to the vicinity of the cruisers, I saw the third CA take a hit aft on the starboard side of the fantail and

Little recognized for the important roles they played in supply and evacuation, the Navy's transport squadrons accomplished a heroic feat during WWII. VR-11 Douglas R5D-3 Skymaster taxis for takeoff at an Okinawan airfield while evacuating wounded men from the island 6 May 1945. *USMC/David Douglas Duncan, courtesy Russ Egnor*

turn to the left, out of formation. She made a complete 360-degree turn and came in aft of the last cruiser, but slowed down. Shortly thereafter I made a dummy run on the lead cruiser from ahead, and temporarily hiding in the broken overcast, I made another run from the starboard bow. I made the pullouts with the bomb bay doors open, to feign a torpedo drop.

I flew back toward the carriers and saw that one of them was listing to port and slowed. According to the axis position, I thought this was White Plains, *but in all the maneuvering the axis rotation must have shifted, for it was* Gambier Bay. *The Jap cruisers had closed to about 10,000 yards on the carriers, and I made another dummy run on the lead cruiser. I fired my .50 cal. (which was all I had) at an elevated angle in hopes of straddling the target.*

I circled around to the port side of the cruiser line again, and they were under a low overcast. I was at about 1,000 feet and between 5,000-6,000 yards away. As I was watching, a TBM completely afire fell in the wake of the last cruiser. I knew that there must be planes above, probably from Taffy Two, so I decided to head for the beach and see if there was any chance of getting a bomb load.

Huxtable landed ashore, spending the night with Army troops. Eventually he reformed VC-10 and deployed again in 1945, with many of the same aircrews. "Hux" retired as a captain, living in his native Arizona until his death in 1985.

With air support from Taffy Two, Rear Admiral Clifton Sprague fought off the overwhelming enemy force in a morning-long slugfest. *Gambier Bay* succumbed to cruiser shellfire, as did some of the destroyers. But Kurita, astonished by the ferocity of the CVE response and mindful of the pummelling he had sustained the day before, called it quits. Just as victory was within his grasp, he disengaged. The invasion transports were safe.

Despite repulsing Kurita's force, Taffy Three remained in peril. That afternoon, 25 October, *St. Lo* (CVE-63) was attacked by a Japanese aircraft which made no visible effort to pull out of its dive. Upon impact the little carrier was wracked by fire and explosions, sinking as first victim of the *kamikazes*. Six other escort carriers were damaged by suicide aircraft about this same time.

Meanwhile, the fast carriers had sunk all four of Ozawa's decoys off Cape Engano. Commander David McCampbell, the *Essex* CAG who established the Allied record by downing nine planes in one mission the day before, helped direct strikes against the nearly empty Japanese carriers. *Lexington* and *Langley* (CVL-27) aircraft wrote the final postscript on the Pearl Harbor episode as VT-19 and VT-44 teamed up to sink *Zuikaku*, last survivor of the six carriers that launched against Hawaii almost three years before. Relieving McCampbell as strike coordinator was Commander Hugh Winters, CAG 19, who witnessed something unique in naval history: He personally saw three carriers sunk.

Aside from the CVE losses, the US Navy wrote off *Princeton* (CVL-23), which was fatally bombed the morning of 24 October. She was the first fast carrier lost since the original *Hornet* at Santa Cruz, and the last such US Navy carrier ever destroyed by enemy action.

In exchange, not only did the Allies gain a firm foothold in the Philippines; Japanese naval strength had been severely depleted. Carrier planes scoured the Philippine waters during 26–27 October, picking off a light cruiser and four destroyers. It brought total enemy losses to 26 combatants, displacing 300,000 tons.

By late 1944, the fast carrier bombing squadrons had worked the bugs out of the SB2C. After prolonged teething problems, both at the factory and in the fleet, the Helldiver came into its own, as recalled by a veteran dive bomber pilot.

Surviving the Beast

Lieutenant Edwin M. Wilson flew two combat tours in VB-11: SBDs from Guadalcanal in 1943 and SB2Cs from *Hornet* (CV-12) in 1944–45. His opinion of the two dive bombers' relative merits is based many missions in the "Slow But Deadly" Dauntless and "The Beast" of a Helldiver.

Bon Homme Richard (CV-31) with Night Air Group 91 embarked steams behind *Hornet* and CVG-17 at the fleet anchorage in Leyte Gulf 12 June 1945. *Hornet* would soon return home as a result of losing 25 feet of her forward flight deck when she encountered a typhoon 4-5 June. *US Navy*

I have been asked many times which I preferred, the Douglas SBD Dauntless or Curtiss SB2C Helldiver. I liked them both, as they brought me back alive. The SBD was easier to handle in a dive, to aim, and to keep the ball centered. If you were in a skid when you released your bomb, the same skid would be in your bomb, thereby reducing chances of a hit. The SBD could also take more flak damage—it was more rugged.

The SB2C had more speed, and it carried more armament. I especially liked the 20mm cannon in each wing, which alternated tracer, armor-piercing, and explosive shells. I did a lot of damage with those guns. As I would make my vertical dive, usually from 10,000 to 12,000 feet, I would fire the cannon all the way down until I released my bomb at about 2,000 feet. As in the SBD, we would black out on pullouts, pulling about five to ten Gs every time. I once pulled thirteen Gs in an SB2C, so it, too was rugged; all it did was ripple the top of the wings.

You would get negative Gs pushing over into your dive. The most negative that I ever pulled was six. Both negative and positive Gs were recorded by an accelerometer. I think we dive bomber pilots had "the right stuff," even though at times much of our blood was in our feet.

I never knew why the SB2C had such a large vertical stabilizer and rudder, as I once flew it without them. On 6 November 1944, I led a strike on Clark Field on Luzon. The day before at Clark, I was on the deck strafing and they shot off my tailhook with small arms fire, so I pulled out higher this time. Just

as I closed my dive brakes and pulled the stick back, blacking out, I heard a loud explosion. The one good thing about radio and engine noise was that it kept you from hearing AA shells exploding. The "word" was that if you heard an explosion, it would be the last thing you would ever hear.

So, as soon as I finished my pullout and my vision returned, I asked my gunner, Harry Jesperson, what happened. "Mr. Wilson," he said, "we have no tail." Apparently, when a 40mm shell exploded, it blew the vertical stabilizer and rudder off the fuselage.

Fortunately, I had pulled out in the direction of our task force. Figuring there must have been a purpose in that large vertical surface, I did not drop a wing or attempt a turn. I set her down near a picket ship, the destroyer Mansfield (DD-728), landing in a wave that broke over us.

I immediately jumped out onto the wing to help "Jes" get the raft out. He was still in ditching position with his arms over his face and head. When I tapped his shoulder, he was really startled; he must have thought I was St. Peter!

Standing on the wing, we inflated the raft and stepped aboard. The SB2C stayed afloat for about forty-five seconds. As there was a 40-knot sea, we had a rough time getting aboard Mansfield. One minute we would be loooking down on it and the next looking up. We finally got aboard. My first "sea command" as CO of a two-man raft was too short to go to my head.

Two days later, Mansfield swung us over to Hornet. I told Commander Braddy, Mansfield's skipper, that Hornet usually swapped 20 gallons of ice cream for a returned Navy pilot and ten gallons for a Marine pilot (though there were no Marine aviators aboard!) So he would not release me until he got his 20 gallons of ice cream."

"Big Ed" Wilson remained in the Navy and rose to rear admiral in the Reserves. He retired to his native San Francisco, occasionally serving as guest lecturer on history cruises to the Pacific Ocean.

For the remainder of the war, the primary threat to the fast carriers was the astonishing variety of *kamikaze* aircraft. Since Santa Cruz, American carriers had been almost entirely safe from conventional air attack, but with the advent of suicide tactics, air defense needed to be 100 percent effective. Naturally, it was not possible, but the effort had to be made.

Therefore, in December 1944 two Marine F4U squadrons boarded *Essex* on short notice. Quickly qualified in carrier landings, and admittedly marginal in instrument flying, VMF-124 and -213

Marine "ordie" maintains .50 cal. machine guns of VMF-511 Vought F4U-1D Corsair assigned to MCVG-1 in *Block Island* (CVE-106) during the battle for Okinawa, 5 Jun 1945. MCVG-1 and *Block Island,* were the first Marine/CVE team to form. *USMC, courtesy Robert J. Cressman*

reinforced Air Group Four—the first of ten Marine squadrons to fly with the Fast Carrier Task Force. Operational losses far outnumbered combat attrition, but what the leathernecks lacked in experience was offset by determination. Other Marine F4U squadrons subsequently flew from *Bennington* (CV-20), *Bunker Hill* (CV-17), *Wasp* (CV-18), and briefly from *Franklin* (CV-13). Additionally, by war's end all-Marine air groups were operating from escort carriers as well.

Off Iwo Jima in February 1945, the aging *Saratoga* took four *kamikazes*. Though knocked out of the war, "Sara" still steamed under her own power. Things only got worse off Okinawa following the invasion of 1 April.

After initial carrier strikes against Tokyo, the fast carriers concentrated on whittling down Japanese air power in the home

islands and Ryukyus. Only a few hundred miles from southern Japan, Okinawa amounted to the empire's doorstep. In order to support the major undertaking of seizing Okinawa, the carriers had to remain in a restricted area usually no more than 100 miles offshore. This requirement solved the enemy's main problem: locating his target. For two months the fast carriers, ably assisted by the CVEs, fought a continuous battle against conventional and suicide air raids in addition to providing ground support for Marines and Army troops.

Four CVE(T)s delivered two Marine air groups to Okinawa in the week following L-Day, 1 April 1945. They flew off 192 Corsairs and 30 Hellcat night fighters for the Tactical Air Force—the first launch being made while under *kamikaze* attack.

Seaplane tender crew prepares to hoist a Martin PBM-5 Mariner from Kerama Retto anchorage for servicing during summer 1945. PBM construction continued until April 1949 and the last Mariners served with VP-50 until July 1956. *US Navy, courtesy Russ Egnor*

The replenishment group was kept fully occupied at its usual job during Operation Iceberg. Four ships of Task Unit 50.8.4 kept the CVs, CVLs, and engaged CVEs supplied with F6Fs, F4Us, SB2Cs, FMs, and TBMs through the entire period of Okinawa support operations. One gauge of the level of activity is the six-week period 14 March to 27 May, when 854 aircraft and 207 aircrew were issued to the fleet at sea. To support such intense operations in WestPac, seventeen CVEs shuttled from the West Coast to forward staging

bases, bringing ever more replacement planes and spares to the replenishment group.

On VJ-Day there were 33 CVE(T)s, including six Royal Navy carriers. CarTransRonPac had ferried 31,700 aircraft during its 15 months of service. They included 4,500 replacement CV planes and an equal number of Army and Marine Corps garrison aircraft. The CVEs also transported thousands of war-weary or obsolescent planes to rear areas or to the United States

Perhaps the greatest tribute to the CVE(T)s came from the enemy. At war's end, former Prime Minister Hideki Tojo identified the reasons for Japan's defeat. He mentioned the island-hopping strategy and US submarine operations, but American ability to sustain carrier task forces at sea for prolonged periods was crucial.

Another unheralded organization was Naval Air Transport Service (NATS) which lifted supplies, equipment, and casualties thousands of miles across the Pacific. Originally contracted to Pan-American Airways, NATS began operations from Alameda, California, on 1 April 1942. By year's end, service extended to Australia as the Navy continued building its own airline.

NATS increased throughout the war, covering the extent of the Pacific from the Aleutians southward. The expansion was, in the words of a Navy report, "phenomenal." In the first half of 1943, NATS logged more than 5,000,000 plane miles. In the last half of 1944, that figure had nearly quadrupled.

Running the Navy's Airline

Captain D.W. "Tommy" Tomlinson graduated from Annapolis in 1916, became an early aviator, and left the service for airline work with TWA. Recalled to active duty, he became Commander Naval Air Transport Service Pacific in 1942, remaining in that capacity almost until the end of the war.

We had several squadrons from the West Coast to the Philippines, with both landplanes and seaplanes. VR-2 was responsible for the PB2Ys at Alameda only. VR-4 was the secondary maintenance squadron at Oakland. In Seattle I had VR-5, which served Alaska. In VR-11, which flew R5Ds, the squadron commander was the landplane chief pilot. At the end of the war he had 3,000 pilots. VR-10 at Honolulu was the system maintenance department, the main overhaul base. It supplied trained mechanics at forward-area stations, and at Guam a special unit of about 1,000 men and six nose docks for R5Ds. At Noumea there was another detachment of VR-10, with about 20 PBMs. It maintained them and operated between Espiritu Santo, Noumea, and Auckland.

Before they were allowed to fly the Pacific, the R5D pilots had special training at Crow's Landing, California. I had two outstanding former TWA pilots there. I told them, "When you check a man out, would you be content, if you brought your family and saw this pilot in the cockpit as captain, and the weather was a little marginal, would you put them aboard the airplane with him? If you wouldn't do that, he is out so far as NATSPac is concerned."

The check pilots were plenty tough. I never got any flare-back, though we weeded out quite a few. After Crow's Landing, they had to put in 100 hours flying cargo across the Pacific before they could fly regular passenger schedules. We lost one cargo R5D at Guam. The pilot encountered exceptionally bad weather at night. It was perfectly understandable.

I always flew on my inspection flights when I went to the Pacific forward areas. I always flew the plane myself. I'd put the captain over in the copilot's seat. It was one of my basic principles: "Do as I do." I had to set the example, and I did. If there was an instrument approach to be made, I always made it. I always made the takeoffs and landings. There were enough of these pilots who rode with me so that word got around that I would not expect any pilot to do anything I would not do myself.

In the Pacific we had 55 Coronado (PB2Y) boats. The best utilization we could obtain with them was about five and a half hours a day per boat. The R5Ds averaged seven and a half hours a day. I was told the best Army ATC C-54 utilization was about three and a half hours. The four-engine Coronados weren't bad-flying airplanes; they were appreciably faster than the Boeing 314. I rode one of the 314s—21 hours from Honolulu to Oakland. With R5Ds we were making it in 10 to 12 hours.

Raddy Radford wanted me to come back to relieve Don Smith as overall commander of NATS in December 1944. There was a star in it. My wife learned I had turned it down and was disappointed. I said, "Look, I've got 30 years service. I receive the same pay I would as a commodore or junior rear admiral, and I'd have to buy a lot of gold lace and a fancy cap. To hell with it."

I got everything I wanted in Hawaii as a captain with four stripes. I had what was needed to get things done. My reputation in aviation was more valuable than rank.

After the war, Tomlinson was assigned to the integrated Military Air Transport Service and, in 1948, served in the Berlin Air Lift. Upon retirement he settled in the Pacific Northwest.

Of special importance was the evacuation of wounded servicemen to rear-area hospitals. In late 1944, the Navy established dedicated VRE (aerial transport evacuation) squadrons flying Douglas R5D Skymasters as long-range aerial ambulances. Aside from specialized aircraft, well-trained flight nurses also were provided to care for casualties en route home. The end of the war happily canceled the VRE program, which had been marked for expansion before the invasion of Japan.

Late 1944 and early 1945 brought some dramatic advancements to carrier capability. The first night air group entered combat in August 1944, early in the Philippine campaign. Air Group 41 flew from *Independence* until January 1945, proving so successful that three CV air groups followed. As noted, *Saratoga* with the day/night Air Group 53 served briefly at Iwo Jima. Night Air Group 90 in *Enterprise* began combat early in the new year under the expert guidance of Commander William I. Martin. An early advocate of night CV operations, Bill Martin exploited the knowledge of Commander Turner Caldwell's Night Air Group 41 and inaugurated the big-deck nocturnal carrier to combat. In addition to night strike, heckler and intruder missions, Martin's TBM-3Es also conducted some of the Navy's earliest electronic warfare missions. The last night carrier unit in combat was Air Group 91 aboard the new Essex-class ship *Bon Homme Richard* (CV-31).

"Egad, It was a Busy Time!"

Lieutenant Commander William N. Leonard served on Vice Admiral McCain's TF 38 staff during 1944–45. An F4F veteran of Coral Sea, Midway, and Guadalcanal, Leonard had seen carrier operations evolve throughout the war. But he also learned of the continuing battle against Army influence in naval affairs, and of the battleship "gun club" influence in task force assignments.

My time in the Fast Carrier staff was from November 1944 to November 1945. When I arrived, Mitscher had just turned TF 38 over to McCain and Company, and the Philippine operation was off and running. General MacArthur was agitating to have TF 38/3rd Fleet operate offshore in continuing support even though he had all of Seventh Fleet and a slew of CVEs dedicated to his mission.

This situation led to lots of "argufying" because when the Fast Carriers are tied to the fixed geography of an ongoing operation, they lose the advantage of speed and become a very attractive target for submarines and the kamikaze boys, who were coming on strong.

Our problem with MacArthur centered on his need for air support, which the Army Air Force was supposed to bring to Leyte by a certain date. Bad weather and other things delayed Army self-sufficiency, so the fallback was to retain the fast CVs on the scene. McCain and his ops officer, Captain Jimmy Thach, wrote fervent dispatches to Halsey to free the CVs and, incidentally, illuminate Army air's failure to keep on schedule. Halsey was with us and reverberated up to Nimitz (TF 38 could not agitate above the fleet level.) We did our duty as Mac requested, but got it logged that the AAF had better sharpen its mobility to agree with the brochures.

So here we were in an interservice hassle and at the same time trying to fight the Japs, dodge typhoons, improve our fleet defense dispositions, get more fighters, sharpen our intelligence to trap more Jap air on the ground, and expand photo recce to this end. Egad, it was a busy time!

Our immediate tactical concerns were two different but onerous types of "winds": naturally occurring typhoons and the man-made variety of Divine Wind kamikaze aircraft. Third Fleet was driven through two of the former—one in mid-December and another in early June '45. The first was the worst; TF 38 lost three destroyers and 800 men in mountainous seas driven by 93-knot winds. Losses were far less in June, though 30-plus ships were damaged.

Kamikazes and conventional bombers caused us plenty of worry. From November 1944, when I joined McCain's staff, until the middle of May 1945, CVs were hit 17 times and CVLs three more. Though none were sunk, we never saw some of those ships again: most notably Franklin, Enterprise, *and* Bunker Hill. *Many of us felt that most of these casualties of wind and war could have been avoided had the carriers not been tied so closely to the Philippines and Okinawa.*

The jaunt into the East China Sea (January 1945) was about the last time Halsey/McCain were free to go after sea targets with promise of worthy results. From then on the CVs were tied to Okinawa and later sicced on shore targets and Japan's infamous "defueled doggo" navy, tied up in Kure and elsewhere. There was clamoring by the surface people to get a whack at action, and we had the spectacle of battleships shelling furniture and bicycle factories while TF 38 provided air cover! Intelligence could not find any significant strategic targets within range of the 16-inchers, and none of the objectives merited an air strike. Some wag on the staff referred to this effort as a WPA make-work project for the black shoes.

Still, to put the ships and planes in position for these actions (in minable waters, surface, and kamikaze traps) was hazardous. We hoped that as time wore on, cool heads might prevail on high and we could work on the targets that really needed treatment in advance of the coming Home Island assault—and do it scientifically.

Fortunately, the A-bomb intruded as the silly season went on and put it all to rest.

After the war, Leonard commanded a squadron, an air group and the carrier *Ranger* (CV-61) early in the Vietnam War. He retired as a rear admiral in Virginia Beach, Virginia.

Fast Carrier Task Force strikes against the Japanese homeland began 16 Feb 1945 when Task Force 58 aircraft hit industrial and military targets on Honshu. Carrier strikes would continue until the cessation of hostilities 15 Aug. Capsized Japanese carrier IJNS *Amagi* at Kure Navy Yard was sunk by US carrier planes. *USAF*

On 7 April, carrier aviators drove a final nail into the coffin of battleship supremacy. *Yamato*, whose sister *Musashi* had been sunk in the Philippines, was ordered to break through to Okinawa, beach herself, and join in the island's defense. She was escorted by a destroyer division and a light cruiser, *Yahagi*.

Subjected to attacks by some 386 carrier aircraft (slightly more than launched against Pearl Harbor), the force was hammered for two and one-half hours. The major damage was inflicted by Avengers and Helldivers, which slammed torpedoes and armor-piercing bombs into the biggest battleship remaining afloat.

CHAPTER
FOUR

THE MENTORS: TRAINING COMMAND

We had to accomplish the twentieth century miracle of training more pilots in a single week than we used to train in a year!
It meant that we had to solve the problem of using mass production methods and still retain the touch of the artisan.
We had the problem of putting an individual into a huge organization—and retaining individuality in the output.
We had to teach thousands of cadets not only to fly, but to fly better than cadets had ever flown before.

Lieutenant John R. Hoyt,
Navy flight instructor

NAVAL AVIATION TRAINING FACED A HUGE CHALLENGE throughout World War II. Thousands of pilots were required for fleet, training, and staff billets, with constant turnover. Additionally, most aviators had to qualify in carrier aircraft at some point. The short version was: the Navy needed to turn civilians into combat-qualified tailhookers in a matter of months.

Added to the fundamental need for pilots were similar numbers of enlisted men as aircrew, mechanics, ordnancemen, meteorologists, and dozens of other specialties.

On 1 December 1941, the Navy had 7,905 student pilots in training. Twelve months later there were four times as many in primary alone. The realities of total war forced acceptance of growing numbers of women as well, and by March 1943 1,050 WAVEs (Women Accepted for Voluntary Enlistment) were under technical training in aviation subjects.

Beautiful view of an NAS Corpus Christi plane captain hand-starting a Stearman N2S-2 as instructor and student wait to engage the engine before a 1943 flight. *US Navy*

Fortunately, the Navy had a cadre of experienced, professional noncommissioned aviators. Designated Naval Aviation Pilots, these men were rated as petty or warrant officers, but possessed significant flying experience. The NAP program had originated in 1932, at a time of budgetary crisis, as a means of filling cockpits without the expense of commissioning all pilots. There were some 850 NAPs by 1941, and most eventually obtained commissions, if only "for the duration." NAPs were most frequently found in patrol or transport squadrons, but they also flew fighters and torpedo planes throughout 1942.

Though the last of the "flying chiefs" retired in 1971, the NAP program remains a landmark of pride and competence in naval aviation.

Among the Navy's growing number of training establishments was Advanced Carrier Training Group, established at NAS San Diego in mid-1941. Flying from the big mat at North Island, ACTG provided operational training for aircrews destined for the fleet. Fighter, scout-bomber, and torpedo plane pilots learned the fundamentals of carrier operations before joining their squadrons. It was an improvement over the previ-

Advanced Carrier Training Group Pacific (ACTG Pac) was formed at San Diego in 1941. It provided gunnery and bombing training as well as field carrier landing practice (FCLP) for CVEs and their air groups working-up for combat in the Pacific. CVE deck crews were also trained by ACTG Pac. SBD-3s on board a Pacific Fleet CVE are identified as belonging to ACTG Pac by their yellow identification markings. A similar unit was established at NAS Norfolk for the Atlantic Fleet. *US Navy, courtesy Stan Piet*

ous system, in which "nugget" aviators depended upon squadron training to become combat qualified. For some, however, it was a major battle just to gain entrance to ACTG.

Before the Battle

First Lieutenant Joseph Jacob Foss had been retained as an instructor at Pensacola and, with few prospects for combat, volunteered for the Marine Corps aerial photography program. Once settled at North Island, he began plotting how to get accepted at ACTG as a means of transferring to fighters.

I'd hardly hung up my hat at VMD-1 before I began bugging the group commander to let me apply to Advanced Carrier Training Group. My photo squadron only had about three SNJs, and I heard we were going to get B-24s and F4F-7s, which were Wildcats with cameras but no guns. I said nuts to that!

So I kept after Colonel Cooley. I said that since we were supposed to get F4F-7s, I should have some training in fighter tactics, though it didn't make any sense. Finally he said, "Sure, go on over and apply to ACTG. But I don't think it'll do any good." Actually, I think he was just glad to get me out of his hair.

That first part of the battle was relatively easy. But the bird running ACTG was a three-stripe Navy commander who had no use for Marines. "They're nothing but trouble," he said. Every time I went to see him, he threw me out of his office.

Well, I was feeling pretty low about then, because I really wanted to get into a fighter squadron. I'd been an instructor at Pensacola and would've done anything to get to a fightin' outfit. I even volunteered for the glider corps, but nothing came of it so I took the photo job when that came along.

The enlisted pilot program originated in 1932 as an economics measure to produce naval pilots without the expense of commissioned officers. By 1941, there were 850 NAPs (Naval Aviation Pilots, as opposed to "Naval Aviators"). Most prewar NAPs were eventually given at least temporary commissions for the duration of the war. Throughout 1942, enlisted pilots could be found in most squadrons, including fighter and torpedo. Later, they were more frequently found in patrol and transport cockpits. The last enlisted pilot retired in 1971. *US Navy, courtesy Stan Piet*

ACTG Pac Avenger pilot taxis to port catapult during training exercises off San Diego. *Matanikau* (CVE-101) provided carrier qualification deck services for the Pacific Fleet during October 1944–July 1945. *US Navy*

As I was leaving the ACTG office, I heard some Navy pilots talking in the hangar. One of them was complaining that he had "the duty" that weekend. Somebody asked him what duty and he said that he was in charge of the funeral detail, which was usually on Saturday. It seemed that a lot of young bucks were getting themselves killed trying to land on a carrier.

That gave me an idea. So I went back to the commander's office, and before he could point at the door and scream "Get out!" I was pleading my case. I said, "Commander, I'll do anything. I'll sweep hangars, I'll empty the trash, I'll even run the funeral detail."

Well, that must've been a new approach for him because he finally let me in. It was one of the best things that

ACTG Pac pilot performs an engine run-up on his Curtiss SB2C-1C Helldiver in preparation for CVE launch c. 1944. *US Navy, courtesy Stan Piet*

ever happened to me. Between 3 June and 19 July I flew 156 hours, mostly in F4Fs. That's over three hours a day, every day. But I got qualified in carrier landings and fighter tactics, and had the highest gunnery score in the class. Boy, I was ready to go!

You know, it's always seemed odd to me that some birds who are sent to fighters don't really want to be there. I've discussed this with some other guys like Bob Galer and Marion Carl, and they've noticed the same thing. I really think that unless you want to get in there and mix it up, you should stay home and drive the bus or something. I learned pretty darn quick that war is not a safe place to be, and you can't make it safe. But you should make it very unsafe *for the enemy.*

I owed a lot to my instructor, Lieutenant Ed Pawka. Later he was a squadron and air group commander, but as far as I'm concerned, his main contribution was teaching me how to fly fighters. He taught us the Thach Weave, which allowed us to keep eyes and guns pointed in each direction all the time. That way, we offset the Zero's performance advantage over the old Wildcat. I've never forgotten what Ed did for me, and I tell him so whenever I see him.

That's the nice thing about living to be an 80-year-old codger like me. You get to tell your friends how much you appreciate them.

In October 1942, Foss was executive officer of VMF-121 on Guadalcanal. Between then and January 1943 he was credited

The relatively new Brewster F2A Buffalo was relegated to the training command even before the United States entered WWII, as Grumman's F4F Wildcat was proving itself as the better fighter. F2A-3 is on a training flight out of NAS Miami, Fla., in 1942. *Pete Peterson*

with 26 victories, earning the Medal of Honor. After the war he rose to brigadier general in the Air National Guard, was twice governor of South Dakota, and president of the National Rifle Association.

Suddenly involved in a shooting war, with a draft system in effect, Navy air power faced the haunting prospect of losing many qualified young men to Army conscription. It was no idle

Grumman's F3F-1 began service in 1936, but by the end of 1939 was already being withdrawn from the fleet and reassigned as station hacks and training aircraft. F3F-1 at NAS Miami c. 1941. *Courtesy Stan Piet*

concern: the Army Air Forces fought a constant battle to prevent the ground forces from tapping its pilot-training pipeline for potential platoon leaders and company commanders.

However, a method was found to preserve the Navy manpower pool. Various deferred entry schemes were enacted, the two most common being the V-1 and V-5 programs (V for volunteer). Both involved college students interested in naval aviation. The V-1 program guaranteed college freshmen and sophomores that they could complete their first two years of study. The majority of these young men were earmarked for flight training. V-5 was an all-aviation program which ensured completion of the first year of college.

Other plans also evolved, including the V-7 program, which permitted a full four years of college prior to commissioning as a deck officer with option to transfer to V-5. Eventually both programs were consolidated into the V-12 program, including many "whitehats" who rose to commissioned status from the ranks.

With a manpower pool assured, the Navy quickly turned to the means of providing quality training to the student fliers. Fortunately, work was already underway at the time of Pearl Harbor. The Civilian Pilot Training Program (later renamed War Training Service) provided 20,000 pilot trainees a year at 92 schools and colleges beginning in July 1942. Contracts with civilian flying schools enabled the prospective airmen to receive initial exposure to aviation and helped substantially to reduce the number of "washouts" at Navy training bases later.

Other civilian contributions included navigator training by commercial airlines, especially Pan American—famous for pioneering long, overwater routes.

Naval flight training involved four stages: preflight, primary, intermediate, and advanced. Preflight was just that, with no flying but intense preparation. This phase consisted of rigorous physical conditioning with constant emphasis on teamwork. An effort was also made to convince future combat pilots that they were training not only to fly, but to fight. In the words of one Navy account, "We were fighting a vicious foe; preflight was to prepare the pilot for this fact, in mind as well as in body."

Five preflight schools were established in 1942, and they worked around the clock. It was almost impossible to cover all the pertinent subjects in the allotted time, but the job was done. Of particular importance to naval aviators was swimming ability, a skill lacking among more than one-fourth of all trainees. Those who failed to learn, failed to fly—it was literally sink or swim. (Unless, of course, a cadet could persuade a buddy to take the swim course for him. Sometimes a barter system applied:

One of the Navy's most versatile training aircraft was North American's SNJ Texan, which evolved from the NJ-1 with initial service at Pensacola in 1937. Later SNJ models served the training command until the mid-'50s. *US Navy*

Left
Colorful early war training command markings are splendidly exhibited on this North American SNJ-1 Texan at NAS Pensacola, Fla., c. 1940. WWII flight training comprised four stages: preflight, primary, intermediate, and advanced. At the beginning of the war, the length of flight training was 11 to 13 months with students receiving 350–380 flight hours. *NASM*

one trainee took a friend's swim test while the other reciprocated on Morse Code.)

In the huge expansion program, primary flight training was moved from Pensacola, Florida, and Corpus Christi, Texas, the traditional hatcheries of naval aviation. Naval Reserve air bases were established to handle the initial training of fleet pilots: a work- and study-crammed three-month course which got the students soloed and acquainted with such techniques as aerobatics and formation flying. The aircraft were Boeing-Stearman N2S and Naval Aircraft Factory N3N biplanes; rugged, easily maintained trainers with tandem seating. The instructor sat up front, communicating with the student via a gosport speaking tube. Some instructors took additional means of education. A lettered notation on the goggles strap might read, "Climb and glide—65 kts." Since the student's forward view ended with the back of the instructor's head, the message was well learned.

Flight training at the beginning of WWII at NAS Pensacola was divided into five squadrons: Squadron One (VN-1D8) primary seaplanes, Squadron Two (VN-2D8) landplanes, Squadron Three (VN-3D8) service landplanes, Squadron Four (VN-4D8) service seaplanes, and Squadron Five (VN-5D8) advanced training. Consolidated PBY-4 of VN-4D8 prepares for takeoff from Pensacola Bay c. 1941. Note crewmember on top of wing. *US Navy, courtesy Stan Piet*

By early 1944 the Navy had ample pilots to meet the anticipated needs for operations. Therefore, those in the training pipeline were reduced to a point marginally above that which would provide for replacement of combat and operational losses. Student naval aviators were reduced from 25,000 to 20,000, and eight training establishments were closed. It came as a blow to the students cut from training, as nearly all would have won their Wings of Gold. Few of these men opted for the chance to return to civilian status, as that inevitably meant being drafted by the Army. What worse fate for a sailor? Most transferred to aircrew training, as a shortage existed there, or opted for commissions as deck officers.

Some of the young men wearing wings of gold were extremely young. During the 1980s it was believed that President George Bush had been the youngest naval aviator of World War II, at 18 years, 11 months, and 27 days. But in 1991, *The Hook* magazine settled the matter after exhaustive research.

Ensign Charles Downey of Downers Grove, Illinois, received his wings on 16 July 1943: aged 18 years, 11 months, and 14 days. His flight training lasted only nine months, including ground school, and he became a dive bomber pilot aboard *Ticonderoga* (CV-14) and *Hancock* (CV-19).

Apparently the youngest Marine aviator was a Texan: Second Lieutenant Norman Payne, Jr. who was winged at 19 years, 2 months. The training program was so streamlined that some youngsters went from high school to combat in 18 months.

FDR Buttons and Horses' Front Ends

John H. Tillman, Jr., learned to fly before the war and was a 19-year-old Oregon State engineering student at the time of Pearl Harbor. Originally intending to enlist in the Royal Canadian Air Force, he hurried back to Portland from Southern California and fetched up at NAS Pasco, Washington, in 1942.

I went through CPT at Nampa, Idaho, with ten other Navy fellows and ten Army. Our Navy and Marine Corps bunch was sent to Pasco, which was a pretty bleak place in southeastern Washington. It had been a railroad town before the war, with some airmail flying, but that was about it. There was no place to go and nothing to do. Mainly it was windy and cold.

The base was brand new; in fact, it wasn't quite finished when we arrived. There was a large concrete mat and three hangars for A, B, and C Flights plus Assembly and Repair. But the gym and base exchange weren't done, though you could get a half cantaloupe with a scoop of ice cream for a dime.

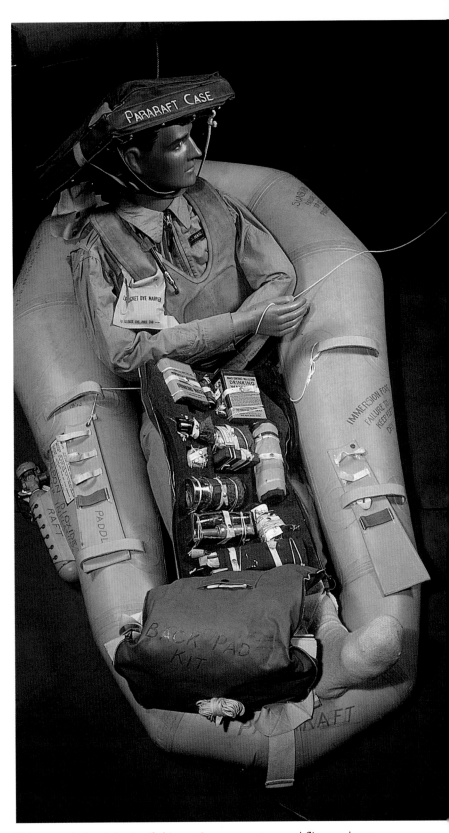

Water survival training is of ultimate importance to naval fliers and was another function of the training command. Exhibit at NAS Pensacola Survival School shows emergency equipment contained in a one-man life raft used by WWII aircrew. *US Navy*

Hollywood went to war and several motion picture stars became aviators. Robert Taylor poses on the wing of an SNJ during his stint as an instructor. Taylor also worked with the Navy's public information section producing WWII documentary and training films. *US Navy, courtesy Jeff Ethell*

Advanced training command pilot prepares to preflight a Grumman F4F Wildcat, c. 1942–43. During spring 1942 the Navy expanded its advanced training from four operational training bases to 12 to facilitate a planned 30,000 pilots-a-year procurement program. *US Navy*

Scuttlebutt was that the Navy bought the land for the air station from the family of the base commander: Captain B.B. Smith. He was kind of a tyrant whose pride and joy was a Beech Staggerwing. The only other one he'd let fly it was a chief NAP. Sometimes when word got out that "BB" was due back in, we'd go down to the flight line to watch him land. It could be pretty hairy.

Pasco was a primary base, mainly with N2S Stearmans. They were a lot different from the way the purists think of

them, with regulation yellow paint schemes. Some were silver-doped, some were silver and yellow, but they were all beat up. There wasn't much commonality, either, since the Stearmans had three kinds of engines: Lycomings, Continentals, and Jacobs. There was at least one groundloop a day, every day. Eventually ten N3Ns were ferried in from NAS Seattle to take up the slack.

The instructors were a mixture of military and civilians, probably with more civilians when I was there. They tended to be

Squadron Four (VN-4D8) Vought OS2U-2 Kingfishers at Pensacola's seaplane ramp in October 1940. In the background are Curtiss SOC Seagulls and two Consolidated P2Ys. *US Navy, courtesy Russ Egnor*

older and more laid back. But I noticed that my two instructors took more time to critique each flight than the Navy pilots.

Practically the first thing they impressed on us was that we were never, ever, to fly over the Hanford area northwest of base. Naturally, that was the worst thing they could have done because practically every cadet who soloed made a beeline for

Hanford, to see what he could see. There was nothing obvious out there—just more sand and sagebrush.

Rumor Control had two theories as to what was going on at Hanford. Republicans said it was a secret factory making Roosevelt campaign buttons. Others said, no, they're making the front ends of horses for shipment to D.C. and final assembly!

Variety of trainers and former combat-type aircraft on NAS Corpus Christi ramp c. March 1942. Aircraft types visible are SNJ-3/5s (foreground), F2As (upper right), F2F/F3Fs (upper center), SBCs, and BT-1s (across top). Some of the former operational aircraft are still in the overall gray fleet paint scheme. *US Navy*

Right
As later models of fleet aircraft were introduced, the older versions often served on with the training command. This SBD-1 is assigned to the Naval Air Operational Training Command where aircrew received advanced training in combat type aircraft before reporting to fleet squadrons. *Douglas, courtesy Harry Gann*

Described by most of its pilots as the "most fun airplane I ever flew," Boeing's F4B began fleet phaseout and training command duties in 1937. They were still in use until May 1941 at NAS Miami. F4B-3 (55) and F4B-4s near NAS Miami c. 1940 wear markings similar to 1930s fleet aircraft. *US Navy*

Right at the end of the war, after the A-bombs, we learned that Hanford was a nuclear research facility. The plutonium for the Nagasaki bomb was processed there.

The base had some enlisted men eligible for flight pay—cooks and whatnot. A lot of them were terrified, because I think we lost three cadets while I was there. One got into a spin, another got clobbered in a landing accident, and I think the other damaged his tailfeathers while dropping rocks on improvised targets. Another guy went berserk, flathatting all over the country, chasing a phone company truck off the road. Finally a bunch of instructors boxed him in and forced him to land. He was gone forthwith; we never heard what happened.

Anyway, as I said, one of our pastimes was dive-bombing with rocks. We'd have some sailor in the back seat jump out at one of the auxiliary fields and pick up three or four good-sized rocks. Then we'd fly out to the Columbia River, which still had small islands before the dams were built. Some of us cadets held bombing contests to see who could come closest to a spot on an island. It was illegal as hell, but nobody seemed to mind as long as you brought your airplane back in one piece.

Jack Tillman later flew SBDs and settled on his family's wheat ranch in Oregon after the war. Between 1967 and 1986 he restored and flew an N3N-3 trainer and an A-24B (SBD-5)

Brewster was no more successful with its SB2A Buccaneer as a Navy aircraft than it was with the F2A Buffalo. Never operational with the fleet, the SB2As went to technical training centers and the Naval Air Operational Training Command at NAS Vero Beach, Fla. Marine Night Fighting Squadron 531 trained in SB2A-4s at Vero Beach before deploying to the Pacific in Lockheed PV-1 Venturas. *US Navy*

Advanced Carrier Training Group Pacific personnel manhandle a Grumman F6F-3 Hellcat aboard a CVE tied up to NAS North Island during mid-1943. As new CVEs were built on the West Coast, they cycled through ACTG for their predeployment training of flight deck crews and air groups. *US Navy, courtesy Russ Egnor*

Dauntless dive bomber. The latter is displayed at the Marine Corps Museum in Quantico, Virginia.

Aircrew training became so efficient that a surplus existed by the summer of 1944. Therefore, cutbacks were made in the pipeline with the heart-breaking result that many competent cadets were dropped from the program. However, six months later the cutbacks were deemed "severe" by BuAer, resulting in a reversal. Aside from increased casualties during intensified combat operations against the Philippines, Formosa, and elsewhere, the operating tempos of carrier air groups aggravated the shortage. Air groups and composite squadrons expected to serve six-month tours became worn out in four, and the Navy concluded that most aircrew were spent after two consecutive deployments.

Consequently, some "deselectees" were invited to reapply for flight training.

Aviation training was consolidated in 1943 under Naval Air Training Command. The new arrangement streamlined the program and added standardization, procurement, and procedures to an extent that required little modification thereafter. Nonflying training continued much as before, but with closer coordination.

Aircraft maintenance was one of the areas most affected by the sudden wartime expansion. In December 1941, for example, fewer than 8,000 sailors were engaged in all phases of aviation technical training. Twelve months later there were over 31,000 in primary technical schools alone. Airframe, powerplant, ordnance, and electronics specialists all had to be provided to fleet units and shore-based support facilities and bases around the world.

Prewar carrier squadrons had their own maintenance personnel, but those were the days when each flattop usually operated its own air group. With the reshuffling and rotation policies required in wartime, it became inefficient to try to arrange for transfer of squadron mechanics to appropriate ships with each deployment. Thus, the Carrier Aircraft Service Unit came into being. Originated in early 1942, by mid-1943 it had gained wide favor. CASUs provided detachments to carriers, in effect becoming part of the ship's company. Incoming squadrons brought some of their own support personnel, but heavy maintenance was performed by detachments (CASDs) as resident specialists.

CASUs operating at forward bases sometimes had a foot in the infantry world as well as aviation. One such unit went ashore on D+4 at Tarawa to prepare for arrival of two fighter squadrons.

Another early wartime innovation was the Aviation Volunteer Specialist program at Quonset Point, Rhode Island. Established in February 1942, the AV(S) rating was just one of a number in the administrative field. Regulars joked that the newcomers commissioned as reservists were "90-day wonders" since they held equal rank with ensigns commissioned after four years at Annapolis.

The temporary nature of AV(S) officers' careers was explained in the slang of the period, uncharitably deciphered as "After Victory, Scram." But the fact remains that the Navy could not have functioned without the thousands of professional and semiprofessional men who became AV(S) officers. Lawyers, accountants, stock brokers, journalists, and college instructors all were represented.

The Quonset Point graduates slated for aviation filled a variety of duties. They became photographic interpreters, intelligence officers, and engineering supervisors. But the most sought-after individuals became fighter-direction officers.

With the advent of radar at sea, control of carrier-based interceptors was a natural progression. Such was the importance attached to the FDO program that at one time it ranked in Navy priority second only to that service's role in delivering the atomic bomb. The Navy therefore received virtual *carte blanche* on prospective FDOs and selected only highly competent prospects.

Since a fighter director is nothing if not a manager, individuals with successful business records were prime candidates. The ability to think spatially, to express oneself clearly, and to remain calm under stress marked the proficient FDO. His training involved wild extremes: from riding tricycles in order to absorb the concepts, to mastering scientific and technical data on radar performance.

Aviation training at all levels was organized and conducted with the time-proven methods tailored to the urgent press of war. Yet the quality of that training remained extremely high, and even fifty years later, Navy veterans of World War II—be they fliers or photographers—still are recognized as among the finest of all time.

As the old saying goes: "The job's not finished until the paperwork is done." Instructor pilot fills out postflight forms as his ENS student stands by. *US Navy, courtesy Russ Egnor*

CHAPTER
FIVE

TWILIGHT OF WAR

The future role of carrier aviation...was defined by Fleet Admiral Ernest J. King when (in 1946) he told a Congressional committee that the Navy's functions and capabilities were not restricted to dealing with seaborne objectives and keeping open overseas supply routes. According to King, the Navy's mission was to deal with "land objectives that can be reached from the sea."
Norman Polmar, *Aircraft Carriers*

THE WORLD'S GREATEST WAR HAD ENDED. OR HAD IT?

Despite seeming evidence to the contrary, for official purposes the "Second World War era" extended 16 months beyond the end of hostilities. For veterans' benefits, for resolution of casualty cases, or perhaps simply because governments abhor loose ends, President Truman declared that World War II extended to 31 December 1946.

Meanwhile, it was time to seal the victory with the stamp of triumph. On 2 September some 1,200 Navy and Army Air Force planes overflew Tokyo Bay following the surrender ceremony aboard the battleship *Missouri* (BB-63). Despite low ceilings and diminished visibility, the aerial parade was final proof to the Japanese people that the war and their empire were lost.

In America, the end of World War II was celebrated in many and varied ways. One of the most unusual occurred in Pendleton, Oregon, two weeks after the surrender.

By mid-1945, the Vought F4U Corsair had augmented the Grumman F6F as the front-line carrier fighter. By 1947, as seen in this photo of CVG-82 ready for launch from *Randolph* (CV-15), the CVG composition on board the Essex-class had changed little since the last days of the war. Seen behind the F4U-4s are Curtiss SB2C-5 Helldivers and Eastern TBM-3E Avengers. *Chuck McCandliss*

Torpedo Planes and Bucking Broncos

Beverly Jean Barrett was a princess on the Pendleton Roundup court in September 1945. During the week-long rodeo, she and her friends became acquainted with some naval aviators who attended the event with all the innovative enthusiasm of Frederick Wakeman's wartime novel, *Shore Leave.*

There had been no roundup in 1942 and 1943, and only a small one in 1944. So the '45 event was the first full-scale event since the war, and a lot of boys were home from the service. It was and is the major event in Umatilla County every year, and my family had been involved since it began in 1909.

On the first day the queen and court rode into the arena, waving to the crowd in the grandstand, and went to the box seats. We were just sitting down when I heard a sudden, loud noise. I turned around just in time to see a Wildcat fighter plane swooping down into the arena and pulling up on the other side. There were American flags all around the top row, so I don't know how the pilot missed any of the poles. He was very low.

We didn't think much of it after that, but later we met a bunch of Navy pilots from Pasco, Washington, about 40 miles

Demobilization after World War II brought drastic reductions to naval air forces. Two Essex-class carriers under construction were canceled, as were 16 CVEs. Spared were two other Essex-class CVs—*Princeton* (CV-37) and *Tarawa* (CV-40)—two new Saipan-class CVLs and three new Midways. The Midway class was designed for a wartime complement of 136 aircraft (they rarely operated with more than 110) and were a vital link in the evolution to the present-day supercarriers. Curtiss SB2C-5 Helldivers of VT-75, a unit of CVBG-75, destined for *Franklin D. Roosevelt* (CVB-42), are at Leeward Field, Guantanamo Bay, Cuba, in 1946. *CAPT Don W. Monson, USN (Ret)*

away. They were just back from the Pacific, where they had flown from a small aircraft carrier, and they were a wild and crazy bunch. They were definitely ready to party.

They sort of attached themselves to us, though the court had escorts as well as a chaperone. I had already met Jack Tillman when he was a flight cadet. I had seen him in his dress whites, leaning against a light pole, and I remember thinking, "Hmmm, how did I miss that?"

Jack had run into the Navy pilots on Main Street in Pendleton, where they had an ammunition case full of ice and beer. Evidently they called their friends at Pasco, because there were several Navy planes parked at Pendleton Army Air Field, where some of Doolittle's Tokyo Raiders had been based in 1942. Pretty soon the blue planes were buzzing all over the county. They buzzed tractors and police cars and everything else. An Avenger torpedo plane even made a dummy attack on a rowboat on McKay Reservoir south of town. I was told that finally the State Police called the base and had them ground everybody until roundup was over.

One evening the roundup court was at the country club for an event. The fliers from Pasco were there in dress blues, because I think some of them had met other local girls. It got to be late and we decided to go to dinner or something, and got up to leave. Then somebody said, "Where's Mack?"

Mack—I think that was his name—was a short, stocky young man. I never did know the full names of any of the fliers

because they came and went so much. But we all knew Mack. Finally somebody found him out behind the club house, asleep under a tree with the club's big Saint Bernard. Mack had drunk 12 Alexanders and apparently crawled through the sprinklers on the green, because his blues were ruined from water and grass stains.

I've often wondered if Mack or any of those other fliers remember that night. But I certainly do!

Beverly Barrett and Jack Tillman were married in Pendleton, Oregon in 1948. They raised three sons on their wheat ranch and still live in Umatilla County.

Officially sanctioned partying continued across America. Immediately after VJ-Day the Navy and Treasury Departments combined in a last war bond drive to help defray the expense of bringing massive numbers of men and material home.

Thus was born the "Victory Squadron" under Lieutenant Commander Willard E. Eder, previously CAG 29 in *Cowpens*. Working with treasury agents, Eder formed a group of combat-experienced Navy and Marine aviators flying three each F6Fs, F7Fs, F4Us, TBMs, and SB2Cs, plus two captured Japanese planes and some utility aircraft. Their orders required them—not merely authorized, but required them—to fly low across the country, put on air shows, conduct "media relations" and party to the wee hours in a different city every other night. In less than two months the Navy's Flying Might program performed 34 shows in 22 states.

Running into early 1946, the Victory Squadron raised $18,000,000. It was a grueling schedule, though the fliers became proficient at waving to the fourth-story stenographic help in metropolitan areas. One flier, notified of the birth of a son, toasted the event with a glass of milk while on tour. Said a squadronmate, "It was the only nonalcoholic drink I saw him take the entire time."

Eder's last performance was at the Miami Air Races in January 1946. Shortly thereafter, the Navy established the Blue Angels under another Hellcat ace, Lieutenant Commander Roy M. Voris, which took up where the Victory Squadron left off.

As with every war, the combatants looked longingly to rapid demobilization. In less than four years, naval aviation had grown beyond all recognition: to a staggering 431,000 Navy and Marine personnel; to nearly 100 aircraft carriers; to nearly 41,000 aircraft. Now those men and women, ships and planes, would have to be cut drastically. By summer of 1946, naval aviation manning levels were only one-fourth of the peak during wartime. If there was some ambivalence, some bittersweet sentiment at parting, it was largely overshadowed by the prospect ratively. Hundreds of perfectly good airplanes were pushed overboard from carriers or dropped off cliffs of Pacific islands. Of 168 air stations and other major aviation sites, only 94 were marked for retention to year's end. Nearly 250 other outlying fields and support facilities also would be closed.

Administrative changes reflected decreased requirements, resulting in consolidation of some commands and functions. In November 1945 Naval Air Training Command (NATC) adopted a streamlined profile, with Operational Training Command and Intermediate Training Command both disestab-

Demobilization brought a boon to the Naval Air Reserve program with a great expansion of air stations, planes, and personnel initiated in July 1946. In November 1949, the Reserve program was expanded to include 311 squadrons under 27 air groups and 27 naval air stations. NARTU Grumman F8F-2 Bearcats are in flight from NAS Glenview, near Chicago, IL., c. 1949. *US Navy*

of aviators, aircrewmen and sailors returning home. Perhaps the best expression came in a popular song of the era:

> *Oh, those who want to be a hero,*
> *they number almost zero.*
> *But those who want to be civilians,*
> *they number in the millions.*

It was no idle sentiment. In a matter of months, aircraft inventories dropped out of sight—literally and figu-

Designed as a jet all-weather fighter for the Navy, Douglas' F3D Skyknight found more success as a Marine night fighter in Korea. It had only limited Navy and carrier service. F3D-1 is on a test flight c. 1949 from NATC Patuxent River. *US Navy courtesy Dick Timm*

Helicopters came to carriers in February 1947, when civilian test pilot Jimmy Viner (shown) brought a Sikorsky hoist-equipped S-51 aboard *Franklin D. Roosevelt* (CVB-42) to demonstrate the helo's capability as a planeguard. Viner made six actual rescues during the cruise and soon all carriers had HO3S-1 versions of the S-51 assigned during deployments. *US Navy*

Early proposals for a Navy jet fighter were not accepted, which led to the Ryan XFR-1 Fireball, a hybrid prop-jet that was first flown 25 Jun 1944. An interim measure, the FR-1 became operational in only one-squadron strength, first with VF-66 during March 1945, then VF-41 when the former squadron was disestablished. The Fireball was abandoned in June 1947. XFR-1 is on a test flight c. 1945–46. *Ryan*

Right
Wartime advances in aviation technology brought about several strange ideas and proposals from Amerca's aircraft designers. A classic example is Vought's V-173 scale prototype for its XF5U-1 proposal. The XF5U never flew. *NASM*

lished. In their place, NATC oversaw three new entities: Naval Air Basic and Advanced Training plus the Naval Air Reserve.

Meanwhile, fleet units began skimming some of the fat with an eye toward retaining more muscle. Two Essexes—*Reprisal* (CV-35) and *Iwo Jima* (CV-46)—were cancelled, as were sixteen CVEs. However, a new *Princeton* (CV-37) and a *Tarawa* (CV-40) were commissioned during 1946, while two Saipan-class CVLs were expected soon thereafter.

Aviation units were reduced even more drastically than carriers and air stations. In the last four months of 1945, the Navy disestablished 21 CVGs, 18 CVLGs, nine CVEGs, and six night air groups. During the new year, 14 more air groups of all types also stood down: a staggering 68 carrier air groups in less than 18 months.

But despite the cutbacks, there was ongoing modernization. The biggest addition to the carrier navy was the three-ship Midway class, two of which had already flown their commissioning pennants. *Midway* (CVB-41) herself and *Franklin D. Roosevelt* (CVB-42) boasted huge, 100-plane air groups with multimission F4U-4 Corsairs and SB2C-5 Helldivers. The third sister, *Coral Sea* (CVB-42), followed in 1947. They would prove long-lived warships, *Midway* remaining until 1992 and "Coral Maru" almost as long. Though in better material condition, *Franklin D. Roosevelt* lasted until 1977. Uncharitably, some aviators snickered that FDR stood for "filthy, dented, and rusty"—an appellation disputed by her engineers. In another example of hindsight, the rush

In an attempt to save its carriers during an interservice squabble with the Army and Air Force over roles and missions, the North American AJ Savage program was developed to get an atomic weapon delivery capability from the CVs. The 10,000lb. bomb requirement of the early atom bombs dictated a large airplane, thus the AJ was never popular with carrier skippers. However, it was successful in getting the Navy into the strategic warfare business. VC-6 AJ-2 aboard *Midway* (CVA-41) in 1955. *LCDR R. Hanft, USN (Ret), courtesy Dave Menard*

The Midway-class carriers were ordered 7 Aug 1942, and *Midway* (CVB-41) was launched 20 Mar 1945, followed by her 10 September commissioning. The first US carrier with an armored flight deck, *Midway* was the largest warship in the world for the first ten years of her service. Two sister ships followed—*Franklin D. Roosevelt* (CVB-42) and *Coral Sea* (CVB-43). Three others that were planned were canceled. *US Navy, courtesy Don S. Montgomery*

Below
Franklin D. Roosevelt (CVB-42) during her 27 Oct 1945 commissioning ceremony at New York Navy Yard. She was 968 feet long and had a full load displacement of 60,100 tons, approximately twice that of her 888-foot long Essex class predecessor. *US Navy, courtesy Russ Egnor*

As a result of demobilization and drastic cutbacks in defense budgets, the Navy's strength fell with an alarming rate. One year after VJ Day, naval air strength had been reduced to less than one-half of its war-end total of 317,000 personnel, including 49,000 pilots. Only 124,000 nonaviatior and 21,500 pilots remained on active duty. At the outbreak of the Korean War in 1950, there were only 10,400 pilots to man 9,422 combat aircraft and a mere seven attack carriers from which to launch. *Bunker Hill* (CV-17) (above, at North Island, Calif.) was mothballed 9 Jan 1947 and never returned to active status. *Robert L. Lawson*

to extreme demobilization would be regretted by national leaders in less than five years with, outbreak of the Korean War in 1950.

In March the familiar designation system for fleet squadrons was changed, consolidating bombing and torpedo units into a generic attack (VA) category. Therefore, Douglas' BT2D-1 became the AD-1. Undoubtedly the most important new aircraft joining the fleet during the year, the long-lived Skyraider joined VA-19A in December. Additionally, the Navy's first important helicopter, Sikorsky's HO3S-1, was originally accepted in November.

A new generation of aircraft made its first flights during 1946, including the Grumman XTB3F-1 (later AF Guardian) submarine hunter-killer and Martin's XP4M-1 patrol plane. Of greater significance were the service's first two jets: North American's XFJ-1 Fury and Vought's XF6U-1 Pirate.

Meanwhile, operational tests progressed with the primitive jets already on hand. On 21 June Lieutenant Commander Jim Davidson landed a McDonnell FD-1 Phantom aboard *Roosevelt*. Later that year, Lieutenant Colonel Marion Carl, flying a modified Lockheed P-80A, continued carrier jet tests.

Helicopters and Jets

In 1945–46, Lieutenant Colonel Marion E. Carl was one of the Navy's original test pilots at NAS Patuxent River, Maryland. With a wealth of combat experience which included Midway, Guadalcanal, and the Solomons, he was eminently qualified to evaluate an astonishing variety of new aircraft.

I had arrived at Pax River in early 1945 and got right into the swing of things at the new Naval Air Test Center. Because I had an engineering degree from Oregon State with an aeronautical option, NATC was a natural assignment for me. My early projects were the F7F Tigercat and F8F Bearcat, but I also checked out in the YP-59, which was the Army's first jet.

The war ended after our class graduated from NATC, but it seemed we had even more to do. I took over the helicopter section in 1946 because I'd had a three-hour checkout and soloed a Sikorsky HNS-1. Shortly thereafter, I turned over the helo section to a Coast Guard lieutenant named Dave Gershowitz, who I regarded as a real pro.

We also got a few captured enemy aircraft, and my favorite was the Messerschmitt 262. As I recall, an Army pilot delivered our first one. Later we got a few Messerschmitt company pilots and mechanics to help maintain the jets. They were hard to keep airworthy because the Jumo engines and hydraulics were so unreliable. The engines were overhauled every eight hours or so, because jet engine metallurgy hadn't progressed very far at that point. Though I liked to fly the 262, I wasn't very sorry when the program ended after my fifth emergency landing.

In late 1945, I delivered a Lockheed P-80 to Patuxent. I picked it up at Muroc Dry Lake, California, which now is Edwards Air Force Base. My primary job at that time was evaluating the Shooting Star's carrier suitability, starting with field carrier landing practice (FCLP). It didn't start out very well, since I had trouble with too high landing speeds that caused problems with the brakes, tires, and tailhook.

The airspeed indicator was calibrated in miles per hour rather than knots, and I found I needed an approach speed of 102 indicated, since the P-80 stalled at 98 mph with gear and flaps down. As with all those early jets, you had to be way ahead of the airplane if you waved off a landing. You could induce a compressor stall if you mishandled the throttle.

However, I got through FCLP in good shape and flew down to Norfolk to conduct actual tests on the Franklin D. Roosevelt. *I spent my 31st birthday making six launches and five landing approaches, including one planned waveoff to see how the P-80 handled. The only problem I encountered was when I got into the ship's burble and my airspeed dropped to 100 mph, only two mph above stall speed.*

We put on several airshows at Pax River, and I had some special routines. My pet Bearcat would be spotted on the catapult and I'd be fired off, pull up into a loop, pop gear and flaps at the top, and land from the down side. It was probably the shortest airshow performance ever, but it was pretty spectacular.

North American's XFJ-1 Fury was first flown 27 Nov 1946. The production model FJ-1 became the first operational jet to operate from a carrier when VF-5A pilots CDR Pete Aurand and LCDR Bob Elder took two of them aboard *Boxer* (CV-21) on 10 Mar 1948. The Screaming Eagles remained the only squadron to fly the straight-wing FJ-1, which was followed by the swept-wing versions of the Fury. *North American*

At one show I made consecutive flights in a P-80 and a helicopter, which helped demonstrate the variety of the work we did at NATC. That was part of the appeal of test flying: the variety and the different challenges. As Commander Turner Caldwell liked to say, flight test was the next best thing to combat.

Carl remained in the Marine Corps, establishing world altitude and speed records in addition to commanding the Corps' first jet squadron and serving as a brigadier general in Vietnam. He retired as a major general in 1973 with nearly 14,000 flight hours, widely regarded as one of the finest aviators of his generation.

While test and development continued, other aviators were demonstrating naval aviation's operational capability. In three days, 29 October to 1 November, a Lockheed P2V-1 Neptune broke the world record for unrefueled flight: 11,235 miles from Perth, Australia, to Columbus, Ohio. The patrol plane, named *Truculent Turtle*, was flown by a very senior crew composed of Commanders T.D. Davies, E.P. Rankin, W.S. Reid, and Lieutenant Commander R.A. Tabeling. Elapsed time was 55 hours, 17 minutes for an average speed of just over 200 knots.

At the other end of the performance spectrum was an NAS Patuxent River effort at the national air races. In Cleveland that November, Lieutenant Commander M.W. Davenport—previously one of Tom Blackburn's VF-17 aces—established an eyewatering record in a combat-configured Bearcat. Including a 115-foot takeoff run he reached 10,000 feet in 94 seconds. "Butch" Davenport's flight set a piston-engine "time to climb" record that stood for decades.

In Operation Frostbite, *Midway* and part of Air Group 74 conducted cold-weather tests in Davis Strait during March. Tests extended above the Arctic Circle with F8F-1 Bearcats and Ryan FR-1 Fireballs, dead-end fighters with both prop and jet propulsion.

Meanwhile, plans were laid for recalling older aircraft types to fleet service. During 1946, CNO established a contingency program for as many as 6,000 aircraft to be removed from storage in an emergency. Additionally, 360 Hellcats were tagged for conversion to remotely controlled drones. Some of them would be put to combat use during the Korean War.

Future aircraft contracts included the Douglas XF3D-1 jet night fighter and North American XAJ-1, intended to give carrier aviation a long-range nuclear attack capability. The latter was especially vital, if the Navy were to retain its offensive viability in the coming independent Air Force battle.

Technical innovations included test of a heliborne dunking sonar, while a joint Army-Navy board decided to investigate the feasibility of putting a satellite in Earth orbit.

Meanwhile, operational commitments still had to be met.

Thirteen Essex- and Midway-class carriers were operational with Navy air groups in the spring 1946, plus two escort carriers. Additionally, six Marine F4U squadrons were allotted to a half-dozen other CVEs. And despite growing concern of checking the aspirations of an avaricious Soviet Union, patrol aviation still had a role to play. Entering 1947, 16 seaplane tenders were still in service, divided approximately evenly between Atlantic and Pacific.

Aside from deployments to cover contingencies in Europe and Asia, carriers brought thousands of troops home.

McDonnell Aircraft Corporation's first Navy aircraft, as well as first operational jet aircraft for any service, was the XFD-1 Phantom (FH-1 after 1946), which had its maiden flight 26 Jan 1945. VF-17A, the only fleet FH-1 squadron, became the first unit to operate jets in squadron strength when they flew from *Saipan* (CVL-48) on 3–5 May 1948. *US Navy/McDonnell, courtesy Don S. Montgomery*

Short conversion periods were necessary in East and West Coast naval yards, installing tiers of bunks and adapting messes and galleys to the needs of swarms of returning GIs.

In the first full year of the Cold War, carriers established a highly visible presence. As a result of Soviet moves against Turkey for access to the Dardanelles, and Kremlin support of Communist insurgents in Greece, US Navy task groups began a string of Mediterranean deployments. Among the first carriers so involved was *Roosevelt*, whose Air Group 75 boasted more offensive potential than any of the region's land-based air forces. Consequently, Navy Secretary James Forrestal established a policy of semipermanent carrier deployments to "the Med." It remains in force today.

The careers of naval aviation veterans during the postwar world included three US presidents. Best known was George Bush, who flew TBMs from *San Jacinto* during 1944. At the same time, Gerald Ford was assistant navigator in *Monterey*, while Richard Nixon served as an aviation supply officer in the Solomons.

Minnesota Senator Joseph McCarthy was an air combat intelligence officer in VMSB-235, the same squadron in which future New York Representative Otis G. Pike flew 80 combat missions. Pike subsequently logged 40 more missions as a night-fighter pilot. Another future congressman, Virginia's Bill Whitehurst, was a *Yorktown* TBM crewman at the end of the war.

As previously noted, Texas Governor and Navy Secretary John Connolly had been a fighter director aboard *Essex*. He was the FDO who vectored CAG-15 onto a large gaggle of bandits over Leyte, resulting in Dave McCampbell's record-setting nine kills in one mission.

Future astronaut and Ohio Senator John Glenn flew Corsairs in the Marshall Islands and in China. Boston Red Sox slugger Ted Williams became a Marine Corps flight instructor before resuming his baseball career, which in turn was interrupted by the Korean War.

Among the genuine Hollywood heroes was Bert Dewayne Morris, best known for his role as Kid Galahad, who became a fighter ace in VF-15. Aircrewman Richard Boone, so lethal as the TV gunfighter Paladin, developed his shooting eye from the turret of an Avenger. And screen idol Tyrone Power flew Marine transport aircraft for a time.

Whatever their later stations in life, the naval aviation veterans of World War II had all contributed to victory.

All Hands: Well Done!

During the massive demobilization of 1945–46, the Secretary of the Navy sent a letter of appreciation to each man who separated from the service. It was a model of pungent brevity:

With the great leaps that were occurring in postwar aviation technology, the mainstay aircraft of WWII quickly became obsolete. Many of these fighting planes were utilized in such roles as trainers and drones. Grumman F6F-3K Hellcat drones at NAS Atlantic City, N.J., 18 Mar 1946, were assigned to Operation Crossroads to fly through the atomic clouds at Bikini to measure radiation. Different colored tails indicated radio frequency of the aircraft. *US Navy*

My dear (rank and name):

I have addressed this letter to reach you after all the formalities of your separation from active service are completed. I have done so because, without formality but as clearly as I know how to say it, I want the Navy's pride in you, which it is my privilege to express, to reach into your civil life and to remain with you always.

You have served in the greatest Navy in the world.

It crushed two enemy fleets at once, receiving their surrenders only four months apart.

It brought our land-based airpower within bombing range of the enemy, and set our ground armies on the beachheads of final victory.

It performed the multitude of tasks necessary to support these military operations.

No other Navy at any time has done so much. For your part in these achievements you deserve to be proud as long as you live. The Nation which you served at a time of crisis will remember you with gratitude.

The best wishes of the Navy go with you into your future life. Good luck!

Sincerely,
James Forrestal

EPILOGUE

WHAT A DIFFERENCE A HALF-CENTURY MAKES.

Naval aviation's major postwar efforts in Korea and Vietnam proved the validity of Admiral King's 1946 prediction that carriers would support land operations. It was especially true during North Korea's 1950 invasion of the south, when US Air Force squadrons withdrew to Japan, leaving only the Navy and Marine Corps to provide on-call tactical airpower for outnumbered GIs and ROKs.

Fifty years after VJ-Day, following Desert Storm, naval aviation is nearly unrecognizable from the organization that fought World War II. The hardware alone is unfathomable by 1945 standards: huge nuclear-powered carriers, supersonic jets, and the now-commonplace helicopter. With no naval adversary worthy of the name, maritime patrol's mission has diminished and carrier air wings concentrate on power projection ashore.

Human factors also have changed. The first thing an *Essex* or *Casablanca* sailor would notice aboard *Eisenhower* (CVN-69) or *Lincoln* (CVN-72) are female aircrew and ship's company. But organizational changes also exist, most notably in the air wing. The World War II air group commander—usually a commander—has been replaced by a captain as "Super CAG" who functions as air warfare advisor to the battle group commander. The deputy or "D-CAG" is more likely to plan and lead air wing combat missions.

Today's aviators and carrier sailors are different than the World War II generation: somewhat older (there were 24-year-old squadron commanders in 1945); generally better educated (college diplomas were unnecessary); probably more professional and vastly safer (the accident rate is infinitesimal compared to the 1940s.) The modern navy also is less motivated and decidedly less well led than "the fleet that came to stay." The result is perpetually lower morale.

The foregoing problems stem from a variety of sources. In the early 1990s, naval aviation suffered three severe blows which adversely affected the service's future for years to come. One was strategic, one was technical, and one was human. Ironically, all three occurred on the watch of a former naval aviator: President George H.W. Bush.

Beginning in 1989, the Soviet Union underwent a rapid disintegration. By 1991 the 70-year-old Russian empire had collapsed into an uneasy Commonwealth of Independent States, and the world's geopolitical map was unalterably changed. Not only the US Navy, but all Free World military forces began a drastic reduction in response to the diminished global threat. In an eerie replay of the post-World War II roles and missions feud, the Navy and Air Force renewed their bomber versus carrier dispute.

Then in 1991, Bush's navy secretary, H. Lawrence Garrett, fired two admirals running a vitally important program, procurement of the A-12 attack aircraft. A large flying wing design incorporating stealth features, the Avenger II would have taken carrier aviation well into the 21st century. With cancellation of the project, which was poorly managed and over budget (as was the new Seawolf submarine), carrier air wings were required to fall back on the F/A-18 Hornet for at least the next two decades. Though versatile, the strike fighter lacked the range, stealthiness, and growth potential of the A-12.

In September 1991, the Tailhook Association's annual Naval Aviation Symposium in Las Vegas, Nevada, featured a two-day debrief on Navy and Marine aviation in the war against Iraq. It was the 35th such event featuring Navy cooperation with the independent association. Secretary Garrett and CNO Admiral Frank Kelso, a submariner, both attended as they had before.

A major political scandal erupted after military and civilian women complained of overt sexual harassment by male aviators in the Las Vegas Hilton. Garrett severed the Navy's three-decade relationship with the Tailhook Association (which was found innocent of wrongdoing by both the Navy and Department of Defense), then began a severely-flawed investigation.

Coming hard on the heels of the controversial Anita Hill-Clarence Thomas hearings in Washington, "Tailhook" became a *cause celebre* for feminists. The long-term result was acceleration of combat status for women; the immediate result was capitulation by the entire civilian and uniformed chain of command in Washington. Some 12,000 Navy and Marine promotions were held up for review, due process was trampled, and a "guilty until proven innocent" mind-set became institutionalized. The Navy's own investigation was deemed so flawed that a separate DoD probe was considered necessary.

An investigative and judicial process that many officers and attorneys insist should have been handled in 60 days lasted more than four years. Cynical junior officers stated that, as an oxymoron, "naval intelligence" had been replaced by "naval leadership."

In fleet squadrons, as throughout the Navy, a blatant double standard evolved. Though some female officers were known to have misbehaved in Las Vegas, none were held to the male standard of behavior. Previously the military academies already had invoked "gender norming" to rate women's performance alongside men's; now the discrepancy widened. Some female aviators' flight records showed that instructors were being doubly and triply lenient, and one of the Navy's first two women F-14 pilots was killed trying to land aboard *Abraham Lincoln* in 1994. Though 31 male Tomcat pilots had died in previous years, the Navy was unable to admit the facts: a dedicated young aviator died in the service of her country, owing to pilot error.

Despite admirals' assertions to the contrary, Navy men said that morale remained so low as to constitute a hazard to navigation for submarines. In fact, three consecutive CNOs came from the submarine community, and hard-core aviators opined that 15 years of "the periscope view" led to the leadership failure. Long known as "the silent service," submarines live by diving deep and hiding; at the time of Desert Storm, no American sub skipper had shot for blood in 45 years. That same mind-set was evident when the Tailhook War kicked off in 1991.

In fairness, however, naval air leadership did little better. With perhaps one or two exceptions, no aviator flag officer stood up to defend his innocent subordinates. It was startling contrast to the principled stance which marked the 1949 "revolt of the admirals" when officers willingly sacrificed their careers in the political arena. Four decades later, that kind of integrity largely had been bred out of the system.

Sadly, in the 1990s, among those most unfairly affected were the female pilots and aircrew who demonstrated competence in the cockpit. Some male aviators harbored lingering resentment toward all women because of the Navy's double standard, though a 1992 editorial by a female captain in *The Hook* magazine astutely stated, "What is really important is our ability to fight the next war." Thus, everyone involved should meet neither male nor female standards, but one professional standard for naval aviators and flight officers—regardless of sex.

That challenge remains to be met. Meanwhile, historians note that the Tailhook War has lasted as long or longer than the Second World War. Veterans of both conflicts compare naval aviation then and now and draw a near-unanimous opinion. The difference, they say, has far less to do with super carriers and jet aircraft. The difference is leadership.

The US Navy now is the most thoroughly politicized of all the armed forces. If further proof is needed, consider the 1994 case of the frigate which honored a civilian imposter posing as a fighter ace and retired admiral. Advised of the sham, the ship's subsequent CO responded that no disrespect was intended "toward our Navy *fighting men and women* of the United States Navy who served in World War II." (Emphasis added.)

Fortunately, there is another difference as well. Fifty years ago, America could not afford trendy political correctness in its armed forces. Too much was at stake, including possibly the future of the Republic itself.

Today, with no overt threat in the world, naval aviation can afford to wallow in its lingering doldrums. Despite the ineptitude and lack of character that marked the A-12 and Tailhook scandals, new carriers are being authorized—but carriers which will deploy with fewer aircraft on their decks. Probably by 1997, for the first time since 1925, the US Navy will have no dedicated attack squadrons. That fact alone speaks volumes.

If there is to be a renaissance in naval aviation leadership, it will have to await a generational change. It can only occur when current officers—whose careers include the post-Cold War Navy—eventually pin on their own stars. But they, unlike their predecessors, will have to remember who they are, where they came from, and why they worked so hard for Wings of Gold.

Meanwhile, the depletion of the "War Two" generation only accelerates. But those men who strapped into Dauntlesses and Hellcats, Catalinas and Privateers—and those who helped put them over the target—can rest easy now. Whatever else happened in their lives, they know an indisputable truth:

When it mattered most, and when the odds were longest, naval aviation prevailed. And in prevailing, it made a difference to the United States of America, and to the world.

INDEX